A
CENTURY OF
HORSE
RACING
MEMORIES

A
CENTURY OF
HORSE
RACING
MEMORIES

DREW SLATER

iUniverse

A CENTURY OF HORSE RACING MEMORIES

iUniverse books may be ordered through booksellers or by contacting:

iUniverse
1663 Liberty Drive
Bloomington, IN 47403
www.iuniverse.com
1-800-Authors (1-800-288-4677)

ISBN: 978-1-5320-6882-9 (sc)
ISBN: 978-1-5320-6883-6 (e)

Library of Congress Control Number: 2019901862

Print information available on the last page.

iUniverse rev. date: 08/13/2019

INTRODUCTION

The twentieth century was the golden age of thoroughbred racing in America. We are unlikely ever to see its like again because the competition is so thin nowadays, due to the horses' infrequent appearances on the track. This unfortunate trend has been growing for decades. In the first half of the twentieth century, ninety-one horses who are included in this book raced more than fifty times. During the second half, that number was down to forty-five, even though there were many more steeds born in the second half. In the forties alone, we were able to list twenty-nine good horses who raced more than fifty times. For the nineties, we were unable to find a single one. Best Pal raced forty-seven times.

We will begin our discussion with an overview of the century, highlighting what was special about each decade. After that, we will get into the details of what was most memorable about racing's golden, unforgettable years. For each decade, we will spotlight the twenty horses who were either the best or the most famous. We will explain what was good about each horse and what, if anything, was not so good. Now they're all in the starting gate – and they're off!

1900 – 1910

During the first decade of the twentieth century, nearly all important racing took place in New York. Such long-gone tracks as Gravesend, Brighton Beach and Sheepshead Bay were flourishing. These tracks closed around 1910, never to be heard from again. However, Belmont Park, which opened in 1905, is still going strong today. There also was racing in some places you wouldn't expect, such as Tennessee and Missouri.

Colin and Sysonby, the two best horses of the decade, both were the property of James R. Keene, the leading owner of the period. There was more emphasis on juvenile racing at that time. The Futurity at Belmont was considered more important than the Kentucky Derby. At the same time, distance events at more than two miles were contested every year. Such marathons are virtually extinct today because horses are not bred for stamina anymore.

1910 – 1920

Racing was banned in New York in 1911 and 1912, focusing the spotlight on other places like Kentucky and Canada. Maryland racing really blossomed in this decade, which saw the openings of Bowie, Havre de Grace and Laurel. The Kentucky Derby became a more important race after the great filly Regret, who was well known in the east, won the event.

Purses were small during this period, causing horses to stay in training longer. Whisk Broom II, Roamer, Borrow, Pennant, Old Rosebud, The Finn, George Smith, Cudgel and sprinters Jack Atkin, Iron Mask and Pan Zareta made the handicap division as strong and deep as it has ever been.

1920 – 1930

This decade is remembered primarily for the incomparable Man o' War, America's greatest thoroughbred. He was easily the most accomplished horse of the decade, but the most popular one may well have been Exterminator, who raced with distinction for many years.

International racing was an unusual feature of the twenties. England's Papyrus came here in 1923 for a match race, which he lost. France's Epinard invaded in 1924 to compete in three specials. He ran second in all three events. Illinois racing burst upon the scene with the openings of Arlington Park and Washington Park, where top eastern horses came to compete and continued to do so until 1970.

1930 – 1940

The Triple Crown came of age during the thirties and was won by three different horses. Prior to this decade, there was no recognized Triple Crown, and no one ever thought about it. Gallant Fox and Omaha were owned by the Belair Stud of William Woodward and trained by Sunny Jim Fitzsimmons. Other important owners included C. V. Whitney, who raced Equipoise; Greentree Stable, which owned Twenty Grand; Alfred G. Vanderbilt, who campaigned Discovery; and Samuel Riddle, who owned War Admiral.

The important tracks of southern California – Santa Anita, Hollywood Park and Del Mar – all opened in the thirties, and Seabiscuit became the first big star of the west coast. Another significant event was the advent of an official poll to determine each year's champions. Prior to 1936, there was a general consensus among horsemen, but no official voting.

1940 – 1950

Triple Crowns continued to be commonplace in the forties, as four new horses added their names to the honor roll. Two of them, Whirlaway and Citation, were owned by the Calumet Farm of Warren Wright. This stable dominated the decade with these stars plus Twilight Tear, Armed, Coaltown, Pensive, Ponder, Two Lea, Bewitch and others.

Match races were popular in the forties, the important ones occurring in 1942 (Alsab vs. Whirlaway), 1947 (Armed vs. Assault) and 1949 (Capot vs. Coaltown). For the first time, fillies were anointed Horse of the Year in 1944 and 1945. Three New Jersey tracks opened in the forties: Atlantic City, Garden State and the modern version of Monmouth Park.

1950 – 1960

Middleground, Mark-Ye-Well, Errard King, Determine, Helioscope, Saratoga, Bardstown, Traffic Judge, Swoon's Son, Gallant Man, Gen. Duke, Vertex, Hillsdale. Not one of these horses ever won a title, yet they were important stars of the fifties, a decade in which the depth of talent may have been the best ever. On top of that, six horses who did win awards were of the highest calibre: Tom Fool, Native Dancer, Nashua, Swaps, Bold Ruler, Round Table. Perhaps the keen competition was the reason why there were no Triple Crown winners in this decade.

Grass racing blossomed in the fifties when the Washington D.C. International was instituted. It was a great era for jockeys, with Eddie Arcaro, Bill Shoemaker and Bill Hartack all in their prime. The best sires were imported horses: Nasrullah, Alibhai, Heliopolis, Khaled and Princequillo.

1960 – 1970

    As in the fifties, there were no Triple Crown winners in the sixties, but no less than five horses had a chance at it. The Derby-Preakness winners were Carry Back, Northern Dancer, Kauai King, Forward Pass and Majestic Prince. All five of them failed in the Belmont.

    Ironically, none of this quintet were the great horses of the decade, which probably explains their failure. The great ones were Kelso, Buckpasser, Damascus and Dr. Fager. The last three of these clashed in the "Race of the Decade," the 1967 Woodward Stakes. The preeminent stud of the sixties was Bold Ruler, who led the sire list for seven straight years.

1970 – 1980

In modern times it is much harder to win the Triple Crown because the foal crops are so much larger than they were in the thirties and forties. Nonetheless, three supremely great horses pulled it off: Secretariat, Seattle Slew and Affirmed. After 1978, no horse swept the Triple Crown for thirty-seven years because no horse was ever great enough. Other much-acclaimed horses of this decade were Forego, Ruffian, Alydar and Spectacular Bid.

A wonderful new race, the Marlboro Cup, was unveiled in the seventies. The Eclipse Awards, the modern format for choosing champions, began in 1971. The grading of stakes races commenced in 1973. But the seventies always will be remembered most for the fabulous horses it gave us.

1980 – 1990

Spectacular Bid, the last of the true superhorses, enjoyed his best year in 1980, and ageless John Henry became the most popular star of the decade. The most momentous event of the eighties was the advent of the Breeders' Cup races, racing's equivalent of the Olympics. Often these showdown events decided championships, as they did in 1989 when Sunday Silence and Easy Goer battled it out in the Classic.

The eighties were the best time ever for female thoroughbreds. Fillies Genuine Risk and Winning Colors won the Kentucky Derby, All Along and Lady's Secret became Horse of the Year, Personal Ensign went undefeated, and Miesque took the Breeders' Cup Mile over colts two years in a row. The most remarkable trainer of the decade was Woody Stephens, who won the Belmont Stakes five consecutive times, 1982-86.

1990 – 1999

The top star of this decade was Cigar, whose winning streak lasted so long that he tied the American record. He won the inaugural edition of the Dubai World Cup, a major new international race in the Middle East. Two years later, another American horse, Silver Charm, took the lucrative World Cup.

The most interesting sophomore may have been the luckless Real Quiet, who lost the Triple Crown by a nose. Both Silver Charm and Real Quiet were trained by Bob Baffert. Another top conditioner, D. Wayne Lukas, won nine spring classics in the nineties: three Derbies, three Preaknesses and three Belmonts. Julie Krone became the most successful woman jockey of the century.

1900 – 1910

IMP was one of the ten greatest race mares of the twentieth century. It's a shame that many people have never heard of her. Racing between 1896 and 1901, Imp ran a staggering 171 times, winning 62 races. Unlike the better-known Gallorette, Imp could match strides with the very best males of her day without benefit of weight advantage. She retired with a higher win percentage than Gallorette, even though she had almost a hundred more starts. Imp carried as much as 135 pounds and won by as much as thirty lengths. Between 1898 and 1901, she ran against other females just three times.

COMMANDO was a very highly regarded colt, considered a champion both in 1900 and 1901, but he seemed to suffer from unsoundness. At two, he easily won five races in a row, but then lost his sixth start as though his past exertions may have taken a toll. Returning at three, he won his first two races convincingly, but he lost his third start and was promptly retired, with only nine races under his belt. His best score was the Carlton Stakes, which he won while conceding fifteen pounds to Blues, who turned out to be a top horse himself. Commando, sire of the great Colin, was the leading sire of 1907.

HERMIS was considered Horse of the Year in 1902 and 1903. He probably was the nation's best horse in 1904 as well, since he defeated the star filly Beldame that year. A good weight carrier, he won twice with 134 pounds and once with 133. He could go any distance, winning at 2 ¼ miles. Hermis was certainly one of the top older horses of his decade, one which was dominated largely by young horses. He won twenty-nine races including nine in a row.

IRISH LAD ran in the same years as Hermis and was one of his most formidable rivals. At least twice he finished ahead of Hermis, but he also finished behind that opponent at least twice. Like Hermis, Irish Lad defeated Beldame in 1904. He also vanquished Ort Wells, who was about equal to her.

Although she lost to the two older males described above, BELDAME won all her other twelve races in 1904, including six against top males. This splendid record was enough to cause experts to consider her Horse of the Year as well as champion three-year-old. At four, Beldame did not fare as well, but sometimes the weights were unfair to her. Her best win was the prestigious Suburban Handicap. She was one of the special females of the twentieth century. She matured earlier than Imp, who was not outstanding until she was five.

AGILE first attracted attention by capturing the 1905 Kentucky Derby. In those early years, most Derby winners were not very consequential, but Agile went on to challenge two of the most important horses in New York. In the Advance Stakes in June, he took on the Queen of the East, Beldame, and whipped her by a nose. In the Brighton Derby in July, he took on the great Sysonby. He proved unable to match strides with the champion and had to settle for second place.

ARTFUL was a very swift filly whose stature was a bit undermined by the fact that she carried such low weight in her two most important victories. In the 1905 Brighton Handicap, she won under just 103 pounds, conquering Beldame, who was burdened with 125. It seems odd that she got into that race under such a feather because it was known by then that she was fast and could carry weight. She had set a world record under 130 pounds in 1904. Also that year, she became, in the Futurity, the only horse ever to beat Sysonby. On this occasion she carried 114 pounds, as against 127 for the champion.

The great SYSONBY seems to have lost some cachet with modern historians, but as recently as the forties he was considered the third best horse ever to race in America, outranked only by Man o' War and Colin. Sysonby won fourteen of fifteen starts in two seasons of racing. He won all nine of his races in 1905, including one triumph at 2 ¼ miles. After he was upset in the 1904 Futurity, it was rumored that he had been drugged by a groom prior to the big race. A number of his toughest opponents were fillies, raising some questions about the quality of the colts he faced, but we know that Agile was a good one, or else he could not have beaten Beldame.

TANYA was the same age as her stablemate Artful, which naturally led to arguments as to which filly was better. Artful had more speed; Tanya had more stamina. In 1905 Tanya became the only filly to win the Belmont Stakes during the twentieth century. She was the event's only female winner between 1868 and 2006. Tanya's Belmont was only ten furlongs, but she later proved she could stay thirteen furlongs by finishing a good second to Sysonby in the Lawrence Realization, a very big race in those days.

ROSEBEN was the premier sprinter of the mid-aught years. In 1906 he set a world record for seven furlongs that lasted forty-one years. He won under the huge impost of 147 pounds four times. He faced the starter 111 times. Roseben's speed was undeniable, but there are questions about the extent of his class. Sprints do not attract fields as good as middle-distance events, which are more lucrative. Rosenben lost the Metropolitan Mile to the average-good colt Glorifier while conceding him just five pounds. Artful defeated this same horse while spotting him eleven pounds.

HAMBURG BELLE was a fleet sprinter who defeated Roseben in 1905 while carrying more weight than he did. By then it was well known that she was an exceptional filly. In 1903 she had captured Belmont's rich Futurity. As a result, she was one of the high-earning females of her era. She was considered a champion in 1903.

After the decline of Roseben, JACK ATKIN took over as the country's top sprinter, reigning from 1908 to 1910. He traveled far and wide, setting track records wherever he went. Altogether he raced 136 times. Jack Atkin appears to have been of a higher class than Roseben. In 1908 he scored a victory over King James, one of the top colts in the superior crop of horses headed by the great Colin.

PETER PAN was considered the champion three-year-old of 1907, the year he won the Belmont and the Dwyer. In the Brighton Handicap, he gave McCarter fourteen pounds and a beating. In the 1908 Excelsior Handicap, Jack Atkin was unable to spot McCarter six pounds. Thus, Peter Pan must have been better than Jack Atkin. After his retirement, Peter Pan became an important stallion. He sired Pennant, who sired

Equipoise, who sired Shut Out, who sired Social Outcast. Peter Pan also fathered Black Toney, sire of Bimelech, Black Helen, Black Maria and Black Servant, the sire of Blue Larkspur.

Soon after Peter Pan left the stage, his stablemate BALLOT carried the baton, sweeping both the First Special and the Second Special, as Beldame had done. Ballot was at one time the fourth leading money-winning horse in American history, surpassed only by Domino, Sysonby and Colin. In the 1908 Suburban Handicap, he defeated Fair Play and King James, as Colin had done. It's a shame that he never ran against Colin. Ballot was the maternal grandfather of the famous sire Bull Lea.

At the time of his retirement, COLIN was considered the greatest champion America had ever produced. As a two-year-old in 1907, Colin ran twelve times and won every race. Unfortunately, he was not very sound because he was only able to run three times in 1908. Again, he won every race. For eighty years, he was the only American horse to complete his career undefeated, except for a few who had hardly any starts. Colin's times were consistently faster than those of Sysonby, and he ran in a more difficult year in terms of the competition faced.

FAIR PLAY was America's leading sire three times. His most famous son was the incomparable Man o' War, but he sired many other famous horses, including the brothers Mad Hatter and Mad Play, and the brothers Chance Play and Chance Shot. He was also the grandsire of Discovery and the broodmare sire of Stagehand and Sun Beau. As a runner, Fair Play was one of the best of 1908. In the Belmont he almost caught Colin, losing by a head. They were fifteen lengths ahead of the third horse, King James. Fair Play won his share of big races after Colin retired.

CELT was a stablemate of Colin and was the same age. When they met in the Flatbush Stakes, Celt was never able to catch Colin despite a weight advantage of fifteen pounds. Celt was a very good horse, though. He defeated Fair Play in the Brooklyn Handicap, as well as older horses. In 1921 Celt was the nation's leading sire. He later became the broodmare sire of Gallant Fox.

KING JAMES had the misfortune of being foaled in the same year as Colin, Celt and Fair Play. In a different year, he might have been a champion three-year-old. He actually did become a champion at four, after Colin had retired, Celt had deteriorated, and Fair Play had been sent to England to race. In the 1909 Ocean Handicap, King James vanquished Jack Atkin, avenging a 1908 defeat by that horse.

MASKETTE became one of only a handful of fillies never to lose a race to another filly. Others in this exclusive club include Regret, Top Flight, Real Delight and Ruffian. Against males, Maskette won four out of nine races, but she was unfairly weighted in some of them. King James defeated her in the 1910 Sheepshead Bay, and she was outrun that same year by Jack Atkin in the Metropolitan. Maskette had been the champion filly in both 1908 and 1909.

FITZ HERBERT won thirty-one of forty-four races, a splendid record for that number of starts. The only horse we could find who bettered that record is Citation, who won thirty-two of forty-five races. In 1909, Fitz Herbert had a season much like that of Buckpasser in 1966. That is to say, he stormed through the year, making off with every prize that wasn't nailed down. In 1910 he took the Brooklyn Handicap under 130 pounds, defeating Olambala (114), who once upset Ballot. Fitz Herbert was considered Horse Of the Year in both 1909 and 1910. He set an American record for 1 5/8 miles in 1909.

CONCERNING THE RATINGS

The ratings of the horses given in this book are based on which animals could outrun which others at fair weights. However, a large majority of the greatest horses never met; therefore, they are graded more on their records and achievements. A great colt should score above 99.

A great filly should get at least 95.8.

The ratings show how good each horse was–not how <u>long</u> he was good. Such admired old warhorses as EXTERMINATOR, STYMIE and SUN BEAU did not receive any extra points for their durability. A horse could run for a dozen years, and it wouldn't make him any faster. By the same token, an animal with only short-term success gets full credit for his best performances because horses can't run faster than they are.

For the most part, juvenile results were ignored. There is frequently a huge difference between how steeds perform at two and how they perform in later years. Our interest is in what horses did between the ages of three and six (or even nine, if they were still good then). MORVICH and TOP FLIGHT had excellent career records because they were undefeated juveniles. However, they did not score particularly high because their ratings are based on what they did at three-not two.

An exception to the above concerns horses who only ran at age two. Since we wanted to include in our book all the great sires, we rated PRINCE JOHN, HAIL TO REASON, STORM CAT, etc. off of their juvenile form because that was all we had to peruse. Whatever one may think of the ratings, the bottom line is: they work. You can pick any year and go through all of the stakes results, and as long as you watch the weights carefully, you will see that the "pecking order" of the horses is exactly as set forth in this book.

1900 – 1905

99.8	Sysonby
96.6	Commando
96.2	Irish Lad
	Hermis
	Agile
	Waterboy
	Kilmarnock
96.0	Gold Heels
	Imp (f.)
	Kinley Mack
	Ethelbert
	Banastar
	Ort Wells
	Beldame (f.)
95.8	Advance Guard
	Shorthose
	Delhi
	Artful (f.)
	Oiseau
95.6	Blues
	Hamburg Belle (f.)
	Molly Brant (f.)
	Bryn Mawr
95.4	Major Daingerfield

Gunfire (f.)

Roseben

Highball

95.2 Africander

95.0 Dolly Spanker (f.)

Broomstick

McChesney

1905 – 1910

100.0	Colin
99.8	Sysonby
98.8	Fitz Herbert
96.8	Ballot
	Celt
96.6	Fair Play
96.4	Peter Pan
96.2	Hessian
96.0	Jack Atkin
	King James
95.8	Brookdale Nymph (f.)
	Maskette (f.)
	Go Between
95.6	McCarter
	Burgomaster
	Sir Huon
95.4	Tanya (f.)
	Running Water (f.)
	The Quail
	Lady Navarre (f.)
	Roseben
95.2	Blandy
	Colonial Girl (f.)
	Nealon

	Accountant
95.0	Dolly Spanker (f.)
	Dandelion
94.8	Ironsides
	Cairngorm

1910 – 1920

In 1911 and 1912, there was no racing in New York, where all the biggest, richest events had always taken place. As a result, American racing suffered a lot and did not really recover until 1914. MERIDIAN was considered Horse of the Year in 1911, but it's doubtful that he was any better than Plate Glass or Zeus, as these horses were beating one another. Meridian was still running in 1914, but by then better horses were competing, and he was no longer very successful.

THE MANAGER was generally regarded as Horse of the Year in 1912, perhaps the least consequential year in racing history. His biggest win came in the Washington Handicap in Maryland, in which he defeated Kentucky Derby winner Worth as well as older horses. It is unclear whether The Manager was really the season's best horse at all. He was not the year's top money winner, and he was beaten in the Latonia Derby by Free Lance.

Racing was more respectable in 1913, but it took a horse imported from Europe to cause that. In England, WHISK BROOM II had managed a third in the prestigious 2,000 Guineas, but he was losing much more often than he was winning. Once he got to America, however, he was invincible. Perhaps he preferred dirt to the grass he had encountered abroad. Whisk Broom II made just three starts and won them all. In the Suburban Handicap, the highlight of his career, he set a world record under 139 pounds! Meridian was in this race, unable to win despite a weight advantage of twenty pounds. Whisk Broom sired Upset, the only horse who ever beat Man o' War.

IRON MASK was the nation's best male sprinter of the decade. In a historic match race held at Juarez, he defeated Pan Zareta, the best female sprinter, by five lengths. In a jaw-dropping performance, this remarkable speedster set a world record for 5 ½ furlongs while lugging 150 pounds! His record remained on the books for thirty years. From a speed standpoint, he was just as impressive as Roseben – perhaps more so – but he did not demonstrate as much class as Jack Atkin.

PAN ZARETA had a longer career than any other famous sprinter. She went postward 151 times and won seventy-six races, a modern record for females. She also set a world speed record that lasted thirty-six years. Pan Zareta won with weight as high as 146 pounds. When you factor in her sex allowance, that amounts to 151! She once outran Ten Point, who was a Kentucky Derby runner-up. Pan Zareta won only six stakes. She was not based in New York, where she would have had more opportunities to run in them.

LUKE McLUKE did not last very long, but he was a very good horse while he was competing. When he won the important Belmont Stakes, he defeated Gainer and Charlestonian, the very same horses that the champion Roamer beat in the Dwyer. In the Carlton Stakes, Luke McLuke bested Stromboli while spotting him thirteen pounds. When Roamer ran against the same rival, the weight gap was never as much as that. In fact, in the 1914 Baltimore Handicap, Stromboli upset Roamer while in receipt of six pounds.

ROAMER was considered Horse of the Year in 1914 and must have been a serious contender for that same honor in 1915. In those two years combined, Roamer won twenty races. He was less dominant after that, but he continued to be a major player in the big stakes events through the age of seven. A gelding, Roamer made a grand total of ninety-eight starts and won about forty percent of his races. He was the first horse to run a mile in less than 1:35.

THE FINN, who was the same age as the great filly Regret and somewhat overshadowed by her, was a fine horse in his own right. He was regarded as the champion three-year-old male of 1915, the year he won the Belmont. The Finn beat Roamer three times in 1916, and in 1917 he defeated George Smith. He was America's leading sire in 1923.

OLD ROSEBUD basically had two separate careers. The second one, consisting of forty-two starts, took place between the ages of eight and eleven. All those races should be tossed out because he was just too old then to be effective anymore. His first career, however, was a glorious one. At ages two and three, he won fourteen of seventeen starts, which was the career record of the great Seattle Slew. After a serious injury, he returned at age six and won fifteen of twenty-one races, which was the career record of the great Busher.

His complete record after age six was twenty-nine wins in thirty-eight starts. No other horse ever equaled that amazing record except the great Citation. Old Rosebud was considered Horse of the Year in 1917, a year in which he beat The Finn, Roamer, Boots, and every other pretender to the throne. He won with 133 pounds twice, and his 1914 Kentucky Derby win by eight lengths was a new track record that lasted seventeen years.

REGRET was the third greatest filly of the twentieth century and the greatest mare. Many people only know that she won the 1915 Kentucky Derby, but her entire career was stellar. At two, Regret won all three of her starts – all of them big stakes and all of them for males. She never ran in a maiden race. Her debut at three was the Derby, for which she was the favorite. For more than a hundred years – 1875 to 1979 – she reigned as the only female Derby winner.

Regret next entered the Saranac Handicap, where she faced a better field than she had encountered in Kentucky. She won again, defeating Trial by Jury while spotting him fourteen pounds on the scale. In contrast, The Finn, the male champion, beat the same horse while conceding just six pounds. After two years, Regret was still undefeated and still had never been in a filly race. Her greatest achievement was the 1917 Brooklyn Handicap. Beaten a nose by a lightly weighted outsider, Regret outran Roamer, Boots, Stromboli and Omar Khayyam in track-record time. Old Rosebud was also in the field, but his weak performance could not have been true. Regret ran just eleven times in four years, winning nine races.

OMAR KHAYYAM and HOURLESS were two evenly matched three-year-olds who vied for supremacy in 1917. After Omar Khayyam won the Kentucky Derby and Hourless won the Belmont, railbirds argued about the relative merits of each horse. They met in the Lawrence Realization, won narrowly by Omar. Sam Hildreth, trainer of Hourless, demanded a do-over, so the two horses clashed again in a special match

23

race at Laurel. Hourless won by one length, and the time was a new track record. To this day, no one is totally sure which horse was better.

FRIAR ROCK, a three-year-old in 1916, was generally regarded as Horse of the Year, but we are a bit skeptical of his ability. In those days, the Scale of Weights gave a huge advantage to youngsters when they took on their elders in a weight-for-age race. Friar Rock beat Roamer and The Finn in the Saratoga Cup, but we are not convinced that he was really better than horses of that calibre. We regard him as equal to Pennant, a good horse that he beat with a mild weight advantage.

GEORGE SMITH, who was named after a famous gambler, was the same age as Friar Rock and won the 1916 Kentucky Derby – but he was at his best in 1918. That year he defeated Roamer in the Excelsior Handicap, but he was behind that rival in the Brooklyn. His greatest performance came in the Bowie Handicap at 1 ½ miles, which he won in track-record time under 130 pounds. It was a "battle of the Derby winners," as Omar Khayyam (just 115 pounds) finished second and Exterminator third.

JOHREN apparently was considered Horse of the Year in 1918, probably based on earnings, but we think Cudgel would have been a better choice. The Travers that year brought out an all-star field in which Johren, winner of the Belmont, was the real hero of the race. He lost by only a neck to Sun Briar while trying to concede the winner six pounds. Preakness winner War Cloud finished third, and Derby winner Exterminator ran fourth, twelve lengths behind Johren. In the Saratoga Cup, Johren beat Roamer.

When Exterminator won the Kentucky Derby in 1918, he was subbing for his more highly regarded stablemate SUN BRIAR. This fine colt defeated Exterminator three times: in the 1918 Travers, the 1919 Delaware and the 1919 Champlain. Sun Briar was a very fast colt who set a track record for a mile at Saratoga. In the stud, he sired such good horses as Pompey and Sun Beau. He was the grandsire of War Admiral's rival Pompoon.

The purse of the Preakness was raised substantially in 1918, making it for the first time a race that was really worth winning. WAR CLOUD captured the first lucrative Preakness, then went on to be second to Johren in the Belmont, and then third behind Sun Briar and Johren in the Travers. War Cloud was beaten by Roamer in the 1918 Pierrepont Handicap. He was one of the high rankers in a superior crop of foals.

Trainer Sam Hildreth considered PURCHASE the most talented horse he ever had, although several of his stars of the twenties (Grey Lag, Zev, Mad Hatter) were more successful. Purchase was the same age as Sir Barton and managed to upset that star in the Dwyer while in receipt of nine pounds. Purchase lost the Saratoga Cup to Exterminator, but he beat War Cloud in the Saratoga Handicap. Since War Cloud outran Exterminator in the Travers, all three horses must have been similar in ability.

CUDGEL was the best horse in the country in 1918 and 1919. He was the third exceptional older horse of the decade, following in the footsteps of Whisk Broom II and Old Rosebud. In 1918 Cudgel won ten handicaps in a row. One of them was the Brooklyn, in which he gave nine pounds to Roamer and seven to George Smith.

In the Susquehanna Handicap that year, Cudgel defeated the three-year-old champion, Johren, while spotting him eleven pounds on the scale. The following year he took the Havre de Grace Handicap, vanquishing Sir Barton, the 1919 three-year-old champion, and Exterminator, whom he whipped three times. One expert considered Cudgel the best horse to race in America between Colin and Man o' War. It's a shame he was never inducted into the Hall of Fame, given that several of his victims did get enshrined.

SIR BARTON in 1919 became racing's first Triple Crown winner. However, other horses were not trying to win it because there was no recognized triple crown at that time. It was unusual to appear in all three races. This explains why there were no other Triple Crown winners in all those years between 1875 and 1930. In 1922, the Kentucky Derby and the Preakness were held on the same day! Sir Barton should be listed with an asterisk because he did not complete the same obstacle course as Gallant Fox, Omaha and the rest. He won the Derby under low weight, and his Preakness and Belmont were at shorter distances than today.

Whether or not Sir Barton's Triple Crown was legitimate, he was a very fine horse anyway. In the 1920 Saratoga Handicap, he conquered Exterminator by two lengths. He lost his famous match race against the great Man o' War by seven lengths, but there was no disgrace in losing to that awesome superhorse. The fact that he was invited to compete shows the esteem in which he was held. The Merchants and Citizens Handicap was Sir Barton's greatest victory. He set a new world record while shouldering 133 pounds.

1910 – 1915

98.8	Fitz Herbert
98.2	Whisk Broom II
97.0	Luke McLuke
96.8	Roamer
96.0	Stromboli
95.8	Free Lance
	Rock View
95.6	The Manager
	Cock o' the Walk
	Iron Mask
	Sweep
95.4	Worth
	Prince Eugene
	Donerail
	Pan Zareta (f.)
95.2	High Private
	Buckhorn
	Flying Fairy (f.)
	Ten Point
95.0	Zeus
	Meridian
	Plate Glass
	Gowell (f.)

94.8   Governor Gray
Olambala
Ocean Bound (f)
Great Britain
94.6   Star Charter
The Turk
Dalmatian

1915 – 1920

98.8	Old Rosebud
98.2	Cudgel
97.4	Sir Barton
97.2	Regret (f.)
97.0	Johren
	The Finn
96.8	Sun Briar
	George Smith
	Roamer
	Boots
96.6	Exterminator
	Purchase
	War Cloud
96.2	Pennant
	Hourless
	Omar Khayyam
	Borrow
	Sunny Slope
	Friar Rock
96.0	Stromboli
	Campfire
	Old Koenig
	Motor Cop
	Jack Hare Jr.

95.8	Trial by Jury
	Naturalist
	The Porter
95.6	Short Grass
	Billy Kelly
95.4	Dodge
	Milkmaid (f.)
95.2	Hodge
	Spur
	Vexatious (f.)
95.0	Ed Crump
94.8	Black Toney

1920 – 1930

MAN o' WAR was more than the best horse of the twenties. He was the greatest American thoroughbred of all time. He was like all of the finest horses of the fifties wrapped into one. He had phenomenal consistency (20-1) like Native Dancer, many speed records like Swaps, record earnings like Nashua and Round Table, and he carried high weight like Tom Fool and Bold Ruler. He was a great sire, topping the list in 1926.

Man o' War set a track record in the Potomac Handicap under 138 pounds. We know of no other case of a three-year-old winning under that much weight over a route distance. He thundered to victory in the Lawrence Realization by one hundred lengths. He defeated a Triple Crown winner, Sir Barton. Some say that a horse of today could not totally dominate the way he did because the foal crops are so much larger now. Even so, in all those years before 1920 when the crops were even smaller, nothing like Man o' War had ever before been seen.

EXTERMINATOR was the epitome of the iron horse, both in durability and in strength. Between 1917 and 1924, he started one hundred times and won fifty races under as much as 138 pounds. In 1922, his best year, he defeated Grey Lag while conceding him nine pounds, and Mad Hatter while spotting him seven. He loved marathons, winning the Saratoga Cup four times. However, we don't think Exterminator's acclaim would be quite so loud if he had come along <u>after</u> Kelso and Forego instead of many years before. His lofty reputation was formed back in the twenties when no one knew that Kelso and Forego were going to completely rewrite the book on what it is possible for an old horse to accomplish. Moreover, John Henry showed that you could be a superstar beyond the age of seven.

In a way, Exterminator became champion by default. In 1918 he lost to Sun Briar, Johren, War Cloud and George Smith. In 1919 he couldn't beat Sun Briar or Cudgel at fair weights. In 1920 he was defeated by Sir Barton. One by one, however, his tormentors retired, leaving him as the last man standing in 1921. Even then, he was not the most impressive horse of the season because of the juvenile star Morvich. It took Exterminator until 1922, when he was seven, to reach the very top. Exterminator was not a very consistent horse. In eight years, he never had a season in which he won as much as sixty percent of his starts. This was not due to conceding weight because his win percentage under high imposts was about the same as his win percentage under low imposts.

Although GREY LAG's status is undermined by the fact that he couldn't handle Exterminator, he was very good nonetheless. Between 1921 and 1923, his best years, he won eighteen of twenty-four starts. He was a good weight carrier too, winning with as much as 135 pounds. Some horses were so indestructible in those days. Grey Lag ran <u>six</u> times in July of 1921 – and he won every race! He set a new Canadian record in the Devonshire International. He was still racing when he was thirteen!

MAD HATTER, a stablemate of Grey Lag, may have been the better of the two. He defeated that horse in the Jockey Club Gold Cup, a marathon race that he won two years in a row. Mad Hatter was in some epic battles with Exterminator, whom he rarely beat. He competed in ninety-eight races, winning about a third of them. His inconsistency was not due to any lack of ability, but rather his volatile personality. He was an extremely temperamental, obstinate horse, very difficult to ride. One jockey found that pulling on the reins would make him go faster!

PRUDERY was the best filly in a superior crop that included Crocus, Bit of White and Careful. In the 1921 Kentucky Derby she managed to finish third behind Behave Yourself and Black Servant. Her greatest triumph came in the Miller Stakes, in which she defeated the good colt Sporting Blood while spotting him twelve pounds on the scale. She ran second to him in the Travers, again giving him weight. A big success as a broodmare, Prudery was the dam of Kentucky Derby winner Whiskery and Preakness hero Victorian.

ZEV became 1923 Horse of the Year and America's leading money winner. He competed in two rich match races, winning both, one against an Epsom Derby winner. He was lucky that 1923 was such a weak year. In 1924 he had to face better horses who were a year younger. He ran fifth in International Special Number One and fourth in Special Number Two. He did not complete in the third Special, but he lost to its winner, Sarazen, in the Averne Handicap. In October of 1924, Zev ran three times in four days – and he won all three races!

WISE COUNSELLOR was the best sprinter of the mid-twenties. Billy Kelly was best in the early twenties, and Osmand was best in the late twenties. Wise Counsellor won the first International Special at six furlongs, with French invader Epinard second and Ladkin third. In the second Special at a mile, Ladkin won with Epinard second and Wise Counsellor third. They thus outran Zev twice.

The very fast CHILHOWEE managed to outhustle Wise Counsellor in an allowance event. He held two American records set at Latonia. In the third Special, Chilhowee tried to sprint with the outstanding Sarazen and got wiped out, finishing last. Actually he probably was the second best horse in the race.

Chilhowee finished second in the 1924 Kentucky Derby after setting the pace. He was overtaken in the stretch by BLACK GOLD. This talented colt is remembered for winning the Louisiana Derby. He actually won a number of different derbies and may well hold the record for the most derbies won in a season. Like Pan Zareta, Black Gold is buried at Fair Grounds in Louisiana.

NELLIE MORSE in 1924 became the last filly of the twentieth century to win the Preakness. She is the only one who won it after 1918, when it first became an important race. The muddy track must have helped her because a better horse, Mad Play, was only able to get third money. Nellie Morse ran second to Princess Doreen in the Kentucky Oaks, but she was conceding five pounds to the winner. She had outrun the Princess in 1923. Unfortunately, the once proud Nellie was unable to hold her form in the long term and faded into obscurity. She was a daughter of Luke McLuke.

PRINCESS DOREEN was probably not as fast as Nellie Morse, but she had a much better career. She made ninety-four starts and won about a third of them, her long career enabling her to become America's leading money-winning female. She won with 133 pounds and often beat colts, but they were not high-ranking males. Her limitations are shown by the fact that she finished behind the average-good Display in the Saratoga Cup. Princess Doreen ran fifth in the third International Special, beaten by Sarazen, Epinard, Mad Play and the average-good Altawood.

SARAZEN was one of the biggest stars of the twenties, an outstanding runner for four years. As a two-year-old he won all ten of his starts, beating older horses twice at that tender age. At three, Sarazen ran the fastest mile and a quarter ever by a three-year-old when he captured the International Special Number Three, the biggest race of 1924. He was considered a three-time champion and a Horse of the Year at least once, perhaps twice.

CRUSADER, a son of Man o' War, became Horse of the Year in 1926, capturing such major races as the Belmont, the Suburban and the Jockey Club Gold Cup. Crusader broke even in two races against Sarazen. In the Havre de Grace Handicap, he won, with Sarazen fourth. In the subsequent Laurel Stakes, however, Sarazen took second and Crusader was fourth. Crusader defeated his biggest sophomore rival, Chance Play, twice, giving him seven pounds the second time.

Crusader gradually deteriorated after 1926, enabling CHANCE PLAY to become the champion older horse of 1927. Most considered him to be Horse of the Year as well that season. Chance Play became an important stallion after his retirement. A son of Fair Play, he led the sire list twice, in 1935 and 1944. His best son was the distance horse Pot o' Luck. He was the broodmare sire of Next Move.

NIMBA was the best filly of the twenties, and there were some who thought that she should have been considered Horse of the Year in 1927, rather than Chance Play. It's too bad that she is not better remembered. When some people say "best," they mean "most successful." When we say "best," we mean "most talented." Nimba won the 1927 Lawrence Realization over Brown Bud, and the 1928 Metropolitan over Chance Shot. Those two colts defeated Whiskery, who beat Peanuts, who beat Display, who beat Princess Doreen, presumably the decade's most successful female.

Another fine filly of this period was BLACK MARIA. She made fifty-two starts and won about a third of them. She ran against colts of a higher calibre than those normally faced by Princess Doreen. Her greatest victory was the 1928 Whitney Stakes, in which she bested

Chance Shot and Whiskery. However, she lost the Saratoga Handicap to Chance Shot, indicating that she was about equal to that colt, who was a Belmont Stakes winner. The above races were ten furlongs, but Black Maria was active in shorter events too. She was probably the second-best miler after Osmand.

Kentucky Derby winner REIGH COUNT, the sire of Count Fleet, was an excellent cup horse. He set a track record in the 1 ¾-mile Saratoga Cup that lasted longer than the race, which was discontinued in the fifties. Not everyone admires Reigh Count, perhaps because he lost more races than he won, but few would deny his ability. In 1929 he went to England to compete in distance races there. He was very successful, winning the Coronation Cup and running second in the prestigious Ascot Gold Cup.

BLUE LARKSPUR won ten of sixteen races in three years, thus averaging only about five starts per season. He was considered Horse of the Year in 1929 and champion older horse of 1930. Blue Larkspur did not have much to beat in 1929, but in 1930 he proved himself by defeating many of the same horses that Reigh Count beat in 1928. Despite a rather short career, Blue Larkspur was the second-highest money winner of the twenties, surpassed only by Zev. He was the broodmare sire of Twilight Tear and Real Delight.

GALLANT FOX in 1930 became the first Triple Crown winner to succeed under the modern conditions of weight and distance. Triple Crowns were won with such frequency in the thirties and forties that it cannot be considered the difficult feat that it is today. Gallant Fox won nine races in 1930 and lost just one on a fluke. Although he had only seventeen starts, he was able to parlay his success into a new money-winning record. Among Triple Crown winners we consider him the ninth best, outranking Whirlaway, Assault, Sir Barton and Omaha.

WHICHONE was an excellent horse who ran second to Gallant Fox in the 1930 Belmont. The third finisher was Questionnaire, another superior runner. Whichone was like Alydar in that he was a consistent winner when he did not have to face his nemesis. He won ten of fourteen starts, which is actually better than Gallant Fox's consistency. He was the champion two-year-old of 1929 and a winner of Belmont's Futurity, which had the richest purse ever awarded in America at that time.

1920 – 1925

101.0	Man o' War
97.4	Sir Barton
96.6	Exterminator
	Sarazen
96.4	Mad Hatter
	Black Gold
96.2	Grey Lag
	Touch Me Not
	Chilhowee
96.0	Black Servant
	Ladkin
	Epinard
	Wise Counsellor
95.8	Naturalist
	The Porter
	Behave Yourself
	In Memorium
	Zev
	Sting
95.6	Paul Jones
	Boniface
	Billy Kelly
	Prudery (f.)
	Whiskaway

	Worthmore
	Mad Play
95.4	Upset
	Milkmaid (f.)
	Crocus (f.)
	Sporting Blood
	Thibodaux
95.2	John P. Grier
	Wildair
	Bit of White (f.)
	Morvich
95.0	Cirrus
	Pillory
	Snob II
94.8	Nellie Morse (f.)
	Cleopatra (f.)
94.6	Princess Doreen (f.)

1925 – 1930

98.2	Gallant Fox
96.6	Crusader
	Sarazen
96.4	Chance Play
96.2	Reigh Count
	Whichone
96.0	Haste
	Espino
	Blue Larkspur
	Victorian
	Questionnaire
95.8	Nimba (f.)
	Bubbling Over
	Mars
	Misstep
	Osmand
	Flying Heels
95.6	American Flag
	Worthmore
	Brown Bud
	Chance Shot
	Pompey
	Black Maria (f.)
	Polydor

Petee-Wrack

95.4   Silver Fox

Whiskery

Genie

Toro

95.2   Peanuts

Diavolo

Sun Beau

94.8   Display

Mike Hall

94.6   Princess Doreen (f.)

1930 – 1940

SUN BEAU was an extremely sound horse whose seventy-four starts enabled him to become the new earnings king, supplanting Gallant Fox. He won forty-five percent of his starts and was held in high esteem at the time of his money record. Eventually, however, other horses like Seabiscuit and Whirlaway passed him in earnings, causing him to lose prestige. Aside from durability, Sun Beau actually was not exceptional at all. He was only the eighth best horse in his own crop, and several horses of other ages were better than he. Sun Beau's favorite race was the Hawthorne Gold Cup, which he won three years in a row.

TWENTY GRAND was the champion three-year-old and Horse of the Year in 1931, the year he set a new track record in the Kentucky Derby that lasted for ten years. In the Saratoga Cup, he trounced the hapless Sun Beau by ten lengths. Twenty Grand first attracted attention in the fall of 1930 when he posted the fastest mile ever run by a two-year-old, nipping Equipoise by a nose in the Kentucky Jockey Club Stakes, a thrilling race similar to the Jaipur-Ridan duel in the 1962 Travers.

Three weeks after that historic race, EQUIPOISE got even by defeating Twenty Grand in a muddy Pimlico Futurity. Both horses were of the highest calibre. Equipoise got injured early in 1931 and did not return to the races until 1932, the year that he set a world record for a mile that lasted seventeen years. Equipoise was considered Horse of the Year in both 1932 and 1933 and champion handicap horse of 1934. The most weight he won with was 135 pounds. His 29-22 career record is almost the same as Round Table's 29-21 record on the dirt. Round Table had more fast clockings; Equipoise had more titles. Equipoise was the leading sire in 1942.

TOP FLIGHT was a very great juvenile filly, but not a great three-year-old. Compare her stats. In 1931 she had a 7-0 record, earned $219,000 and won all of her races against males. In 1932 she had a 5-4 record, earned just $56,000 and lost all her races against males, even though 1932 was not a very strong year for colts. In the Wood Memorial, Top Flight finished behind Economic, who ran second to Burgoo King in the Kentucky Derby. In the Arlington Oaks, she defeated Evening, who was the first female winner of the Flamingo.

Sometimes the best colts are slow to develop. In 1933 it looked as if the male juveniles were not very good, as fillies Bazaar, Wise Daughter and Mata Hari kept beating them. That perception changed in 1934, when CAVALCADE, Discovery and High Quest blossomed into really fine colts. Cavalcade was anointed Horse of the Year, although he did not run against older horses, the most formidable one being Equipoise. Cavalcade beat his talented rival Discovery six times in 1934, including the American Derby, in which he gave that adversary eight pounds.

HIGH QUEST, a stablemate of Cavalcade, nosed out that rival in an exciting Preakness, with Discovery running third. High Quest was not named champion because he did not participate in enough big events, but he was always better than Cavalcade, whom he had defeated in the Eastern Shore Handicap in 1933. He also beat Discovery twice that year. High Quest was a son of Sir Gallahad III, who had fathered Gallant Fox and was the leading sire at that time.

DISCOVERY was a handicap champion twice and a Horse of the Year in 1935. He posted a new American record in the Brooklyn Handicap, a race he won three years in a row. Omaha ran third that day, beaten by twelve lengths. Just a week later, Discovery won the Detroit Challenge Cup by thirty lengths, equaling the track record. He later won the Merchants and Citizens Handicap under 139 pounds, a staggering impost for a four-year-old. Discovery was the broodmare sire of Native Dancer and Bold Ruler – sensational runners and hugely influential sires.

Because he was wiped out by Discovery in 1935, OMAHA is the only Triple Crown winner who was not considered Horse of the Year. He also is the only one who was sired by another Triple Crown winner, Gallant Fox. Omaha actually ran faster than his sire in all three spring classics because he encountered faster paces. The pace was still faster in the Arlington Classic, enabling him to set a swift track record. In 1936 Omaha raced in England where, like Reigh Count, he finished second in the Ascot Gold Cup, losing by a nose.

BLACK HELEN was the best three-year-old filly of the thirties, more impressive than Top Flight. When she won the Flamingo, she defeated Roman Soldier, who ran second to Omaha in the Kentucky Derby. When she won the Maryland Handicap, she beat Firethorn, the runner-up in the Preakness and Belmont! He had the worst of the weights, but it shows the kind of company she could keep. Black Helen had a fine record, winning fifteen of twenty-two starts.

ROSEMONT was the ultimate giant killer in racing history! Every year, he upset the apple cart in some way. In the 1934 Eastern Shore Stakes, he upset Nellie Flag, the queen of the juveniles. In the 1935 Withers Stakes, he surprised Omaha, interrupting the latter's Triple Crown quest. In 1936 he upset Discovery in the Narragansett Special while in receipt of nine pounds. In the rich 1937 Santa Anita Handicap, he defeated Seabiscuit. The latter had not yet fully blossomed and was not expected to win, but it still was one of Rosemont's greatest victories.

MYRTLEWOOD, a daughter of Blue Larkspur, was the most celebrated sprinter of the thirties, busting stopwatches wherever she went. She was in two 1935 match races against Clang, a male who once held two world records. Both races were decided by a nose, with each horse winning once. However, Myrtlewood did not receive the three-pound sex allowance to which she ought to have been entitled. She actually beat Clang several times.

Myrtlewood ran mostly in Illinois and Kentucky, where the competition was softer than what she would have faced in the east. We doubt that she was as good as Sation, the best sprinter in New York. He once tried to concede Clang twenty-two pounds! Myrtlewood had the same won-lost record as Black Helen, but of course she was not facing opponents of the same calibre. After her retirement, she became an important, foundational broodmare.

GRANVILLE dominated the second half of 1936 and was voted Horse of the Year. He swept the Belmont, Travers and other big stakes but really wasn't beating much. He did defeat Discovery in the Saratoga

Cup, but the latter lost a shoe in the race, which probably hurt his chances. It is also possible that Discovery was not suited for marathon racing. He was much more impressive than Granville at distances he could handle. Granville was a son of Gallant Fox.

BOLD VENTURE in 1936 became the second horse, following Burgoo King, to capture both the Kentucky Derby and Preakness and then be unable to suit up for the Belmont due to injury. Bold Venture made only three starts that year, but he won them all. In the Preakness he defeated Granville and, although the finish was close, we believe Bold Venture was indeed the better horse because he also bested Granville when they were two. Although he was unable to finish the Triple Crown, he sired Assault, who did complete the sweep ten years later.

Greatness is not a word to be tossed around lightly, but by almost anyone's measure, WAR ADMIRAL, Man o' War's best son, was a great one. How many great American horses were there? We believe there were about twenty, which is an average of one great horse every five years. We don't think there were any great horses after Spectacular Bid in 1980. (This does not count the twenty-first century.)

A great horse usually has a great record, and War Admiral was no exception, winning twenty-one of twenty-six starts. Beyond his unimportant juvenile season, he won eighteen and lost two. His longest winning streak was eleven races. War Admiral swept the Triple Crown in 1937. He stumbled and hurt himself in the Belmont, but he won the race anyway, equaling the American record. Among Triple Crown winners, we consider War Admiral the sixth best, ranking between Count Fleet and American Pharoah. He was America's leading sire in 1945.

SEABISCUIT was Horse of the Year in 1938 and handicap champion in 1937. He won thirty-three races and set eleven track records, thus running in record time every third time he won. He scored twice under 133 pounds. This tireless warhorse is probably best remembered for the 1938 Pimlico Special. In this famous match race, Seabiscuit whipped War Admiral decisively by four lengths, stamping him forever as one of America's great horses.

Another aspect of Seabiscuit's saga was his four-year quest to capture the rich and prestigious Santa Anita Handicap. When he lost by a nose in 1937, he had not yet developed, which you can tell from the fact that he carried only 114 pounds and went off at odds of better than 6 to 1. 1938 was a real heartbreaker! Lugging 130 pounds, Seabiscuit again lost by a nose, this time to the good colt Stagehand, who carried only 100 pounds. Pompoon, who had been second twice to War Admiral, finished third. Seabiscuit had to skip the "Big Cap" in 1939, but in 1940 he finally won it, setting a track record and becoming the new world's leading money winning thoroughbred. His sire was obscure, but his grandsires were Man o' War and Whisk Broom II.

STAGEHAND was the champion three-year-old of 1938. His record that year was spotty, but we know he was a good horse because he was able to beat Pompoon in track-record time. Slow to develop, Stagehand lost his first nine races. He prepped for the Santa Anita Handicap by winning the Santa Anita Derby over Dauber, who went on to capture the Preakness.

BULL LEA is included in our equine profiles because he became such a famous sire that readers might be curious about him. He was the fourth best horse in his crop, outranked by Stagehand, Kayak II and Lawrin. Bull Lea beat Stagehand twice, but both times with a big weight advantage. When they met in the McLennan Handicap at more reasonable weights, Stagehand won. Bull Lea was one of the greatest sires of all time. His kids include Citation, Twilight Tear, Armed, Coaltown, Gen. Duke, Bewitch, Two Lea, Next Move, Real Delight, Mark-Ye-Well and Iron Liege. He headed the sire list five times.

CHALLEDON was good enough to be named Horse of the Year both in 1939 and 1940, even though he actually was only the third best horse his age. He always suited up for the fall events that impress the voters, who often forget what happened in spring and summer. Challedon won the Preakness and two runnings of the Pimlico Special. His best race may have been the 1940 Hollywood Gold Cup, in which he set a track record under 133 pounds. He also set one world record.

We consider JOHNSTOWN the best horse foaled in 1936, although a case can be made for Eight Thirty. These two horses met several times but never conclusively. Neither horse ever won a title because Challedon made off with all the awards. All three horses are in the Hall of Fame.

Johnstown totally wiped out Challedon twice – by eight lengths in the Kentucky Derby and by seven lengths in the Dwyer. He was the maternal grandsire of Nashua and Hillsdale.

There is overwhelming evidence that EIGHT THIRTY was a better horse than Challedon. He defeated that rival in the 1940 Massachusetts Handicap, with the weights not very different. Moreover, in that race Eight Thirty successfully spotted Hash eleven pounds. Yet, in the Narragansett Special, Challedon was unable to concede eight pounds to Hash. In the 1939 Massachusetts Handicap, Challedon was outrun by Pompoon. However, Eight Thirty defeated Pompoon in the Wilson Stakes. Both he and Johnstown had winning records, but Challedon had a losing record. Eight Thirty was the broodmare sire of 1962 champion Jaipur.

1930 – 1935

98.4	Equipoise
	Twenty Grand
98.2	High Quest
98.0	Cavalcade
97.8	Discovery
97.4	King Saxon
97.2	Omaha
95.8	Flying Heels
	Dark Secret
95.6	Jack High
	Faireno
95.4	Jamestown
	Burgoo King
95.2	Azucar
	Sation
	Gallant Sir
	Economic
	Sun Beau
95.0	Time Supply
	Mr. Khayyam
	Ladysman
	Tambour (f.)
	Top Flight (f.)

94.8   Mike Hall
        Gusto
        Tred Avon (f.)
        Evening (f.)

94.6   Mate
        Stepenfetchit

1935 – 1940

99.4	Seabiscuit
99.2	War Admiral
97.8	Discovery
96.6	Johnstown
96.4	Bold Venture
	Stagehand
	Eight Thirty
96.2	Granville
	Pompoon
96.0	Firethorn
	Challedon
95.8	Head Play
	Rosemont
	Black Helen (f.)
	Kayak II
95.6	Roman Soldier
	Lawrin
	Gilded Knight
95.4	Top Row
	Bull Lea
	Dauber
	Lovely Night
	Sun Lover
95.2	Azucar

Sation

Cravat

Isolater

Hash

95.0 Time Supply

Good Gamble (f.)

Myrtlewood (f.)

Menow

Fair Knightess (f.)

94.8 Sun Teddy

Clang

Thanksgiving

Snark

94.6 Where Away

Marica (f.)

Fighting Fox

Aneroid

94.4 Count Arthur

Esposa (f.)

1940 – 1950

The very popular and spectacularly successful WHIRLAWAY became a Triple Crown winner, a world's leading money winner, and a Horse of the Year in both 1941 and 1942. His track-record time for the Kentucky Derby lasted for twenty-one years. Whirlaway won under 130 pounds but never more than that. Although he was not a very consistent winner, he was out of the money only four times in sixty starts. We prefer Gallant Fox over Whirlaway because the former was totally dominant in 1930, whereas the latter had trouble beating at least four adversaries. In fact, he had a losing record against some of them.

The first horse to give Whirlaway a problem was OUR BOOTS. This talented horse finished ahead of Whirlaway three out of four times in 1940 when they were two. They met for a fifth time in the 1941 Blue Grass Stakes, and Our Boots scored by six lengths! Unfortunately, he was a fragile horse who could not hold his form over the long term. Our Boots had one last hurrah in the Yankee Handicap, defeating Market Wise. After that, he slid into obscurity and was never again a factor.

The next horse to give Whirlaway trouble was MARKET WISE. He finished third behind Whirlaway in the Kentucky Derby. Even if he had run a better race, it seems unlikely that he could have caught Whirlaway, who won by eight lengths in record time. Next the two rivals met in the Dwyer, and Whirlaway again was victorious.

The Jockey Club Gold Cup was Market Wise's opportunity for revenge! After a bitter battle, he won by a nose in American-record time. It was a great victory, but this race might be an anomaly because of the freakishly long distance. The final clash came in the 1942 Suburban. Market Wise won, but he was in receipt of five pounds, indicating that Whirlaway was considered the better horse. In 1943, with Whirlaway finally retired, Market Wise was voted co-champion of the handicap division.

The third horse to give Whirlaway a scare was DEVIL DIVER. In the Phoenix Handicap, their only meeting, this gifted horse held off Whirlaway's late charge to win by a head. Devil Diver won a sprint under 140 pounds when he was only three. He was a champion older horse twice, in 1943 and 1944. In the 1945 Suburban, he won under 132 pounds, defeating Stymie, who carried only 119. Devil Diver was the broodmare sire of the sixties speedster Native Diver.

The fourth horse to give Whirlaway fits was the 1942 sophomore champion ALSAB. This quality horse met Whirlaway three times. The first clash was a match race won by a nose by Alsab. The next meeting was the Jockey Club Gold Cup, won by Whirlaway by ¾ of a length. The final confrontation was the New York Handicap. Alsab won this one, but he had an advantage in the weights. Thus, the two horses came out about the same. Alsab had been a two-year-old champion. A busy campaigner, he made 51 starts in about three years.

People always think that the older division is better than the three-year-olds. This notion helped Alsab win the title, but actually the sophomore division was very strong in 1942. Some felt that SHUT OUT ought to have been voted champion. Shut Out defeated Alsab in both the Kentucky Derby and the Belmont. He also won more money during 1942 than either Alsab or Whirlaway, and he had a higher win percentage than either of them. Shut Out, a son of Equipoise, and Devil Diver were stablemates. They were the same age and occasionally ran coupled.

On the Experimental Handicap of 1942-43, COUNT FLEET was given 132 pounds, the highest weight ever assigned. In the 1942 Champagne Stakes, he set a world record for the fastest time ever posted by a juvenile. A Triple Crown winner, Count Fleet was in some respects like Secretariat. His 16-5 record was the same as Secretariat's, and his 25-length romp in the Belmont calls to mind Secretariat's 31-length blowout. But unlike Secretariat, Count Fleet never ran against older horses and had nothing to beat in his own crop. There was no Sham or Alydar to challenge him. Count Fleet became America's leading sire in 1951.

Since the advent of official balloting in 1936, no filly had been voted Horse of the Year. In 1944 the great TWILIGHT TEAR changed that. She won fourteen of seventeen starts that year, including eleven victories in a row. In the Pimlico Special, she defeated the older male champion Devil Diver. Her time for the Pimlico Special was faster than Whirlaway's Preakness. Same distance, same track. Her time for the Arlington Classic was faster than Whirlaway's American Derby. Same distance, same track. Was Twilight Tear better than Whirlaway? She did beat Devil Diver, and Devil Diver did beat Whirlaway. Twilight Tear was the dam of fifties star Bardstown.

Sometimes a rarity repeats itself. The 1945 Horse of the Year was another filly, the great BUSHER, a daughter of War Admiral. She won ten of thirteen starts, her only losses occurring when unfair weights killed her chances. In the Washington Park Handicap, she defeated the older male star Armed in track-record time. Busher, Twilight Tear and Regret all beat a male champion who is in the Hall of Fame. Zenyatta and Rachel Alexandra beat the best males that were around, but they were not Hall of Fame calibre like Armed, Devil Diver and Roamer.

ASSAULT was Horse of the Year in 1946 on the strength of his Triple Crown sweep. Like Sir Barton and Omaha, Assault lost more races than he won. However, he was not really an inconsistent horse. He was a <u>streaky</u> horse, due to recurring physical problems. During one healthy period, he won seven races in a row. Assault's greatest win was the 1947 Butler Handicap. He scored in this event under 135 pounds, conceding nine pounds to runner-up Stymie and eighteen pounds to Gallorette. His performance was hailed as the most courageous of the year. Assault's broodmare sire was Equipoise.

ARMED was Horse of the Year in 1947 and champion older horse of 1946. He won twelve races under 130 pounds. Many people don't know that Armed beat Assault twice. The first occasion was their famous match race of 1947. The next year they clashed again in the Widener Handicap. Feather-weighted nobodies grabbed the first three placings. Armed and Assault finished fourth and fifth respectively, each one carrying 130 pounds.

We consider Armed a better horse than Whirlaway. From 1945 through 1947, Armed's peak years in the handicap division, he won thirty-two races and lost eighteen, despite habitually giving away weight. Whirlaway's career record was thirty-two wins and twenty-eight losses, and that includes his earlier starts when he didn't have to concede weight. Moreover, Whirlaway never beat a Triple Crown winner. We don't think historians give Armed as much credit as he deserves.

During 1947, Armed, Assault and STYMIE took turns being the world's leading money winner. Stymie, who had so many starts (131), ultimately won the money contest, but he was not nearly as talented as the other two. Stymie was very similar in ability to Pavot, a good horse but not a really exceptional one like Armed or Assault. Pavot and Stymie beat each other more than once. Stymie was named champion handicap horse of 1945 only because he was the most successful at the moderate weights he carried. Some people romanticized Stymie because he had begun his career in claiming races. Despite his huge number of starts, Stymie was not a gelding.

GALLORETTE is often called one of the three or four greatest mares of the twentieth century – and it's simply not true! In order to beat a colt of some stature, like Stymie or Pavot, she regularly needed a weight advantage of nine or ten pounds. What's more relevant is what she could do at <u>fair</u> weights. She lost to First Fiddle, Jeep, Fighting Step, But Why Not, Conniver, First Flight and Miss Request – all at fair weights.

You'd think people would get a clue just from Gallorette's record. She won less than thirty percent of her starts! Is that the record of a great horse? She won only one title in five years. In the other four years, there were always one or two better females who grabbed the awards. How could she be one of the greatest of a whole century when she was not even at the top of the heap in her own era? Despite our disclaimers, Gallorette did have a very successful career from a monetary standpoint. She made the most of her limited ability, and for that she should be applauded.

LUCKY DRAW was one of the fastest speed horses of the mid-forties. In 1946 he set five track records and equaled one world record. He beat Stymie five times during his career, and he trounced Gallorette by twelve lengths. Yet Stymie and Gallorette are still very well known, while poor Lucky Draw has been totally forgotten. In the Westchester

Handicap, he was overtaken and beaten by Assault. This illustrates the folly of pure speed handicapping. Assault never had a track record in his life, yet he had no trouble beating Lucky Draw anyway. Assault was just of a much higher class than his rival.

CITATION is always counted as one of the three or four greatest horses in American history – and rightly so. In 1948 he swept the Triple Crown, and by year's end he boasted a phenomenal two-year record of twenty-seven wins in twenty-nine starts. He did not run at all in 1949 due to injury. When he returned to the races in 1950, he was not as consistent because he had to concede huge poundage in the handicaps. Yet he achieved two important milestones that year:

In January he won his sixteenth race in a row, setting a twentieth century record for consecutive victories. In June he set a world speed record for a mile. Citation's big quest was to become the first equine millionaire in history. He achieved this goal in July of 1951. We consider Citation the greatest Triple Crown winner, followed by Secretariat, Seattle Slew, Affirmed and Count Fleet.

COALTOWN was Citation's stablemate of the same age, the champion handicap horse of 1949. Although never able to beat Citation, he had no trouble beating almost everything else. Coaltown had great speed and nearly always set the pace in his races. During 1949 he posted three track records and one world record. He won twelve out of thirteen races over a period of seven months, carrying 130 pounds to victory seven times.

Coaltown was an overwhelming favorite when he took on three-year-old CAPOT in the 1949 Sysonby Mile. Coaltown took a short lead, but Capot forced the pace with such tenacity that he knocked out Coaltown and won by a length and a half. In a rematch in the Pimlco Special, Capot won by twelve lengths and went on to be crowned Horse of the Year. One should not take a horse's win percentage too seriously. Coaltown was a lot more consistent than Capot, but he still couldn't beat him. Capot was a top-class horse who had won the Preakness and the Belmont.

NOOR beat Citation four times in 1950, but the weights were only fair in their last meeting, by which time Citation was hurting physically. Their most memorable duel was the fourteen-furlong San

Juan Capistrano, won by a nose by Noor, who was in receipt of thirteen pounds. The leading three-year-old, Hill Prince, defeated Noor in New York, but Noor got even in the Hollywood Gold Cup. In that race, Noor gave Palestinian eight pounds and a thrashing. Capot had been unable to give Palestinian five pounds in the 1949 Empire City Handicap. Thus, Noor must have been better than Capot. He set two world records, one American record, and three track records in 1950.

NEXT MOVE was a champion at three and at five. At three she defeated the high-earning mare Bewitch in the 1950 Vanity Handicap. In the Hollywood Gold Cup, she finished fourth of eight, beaten by Noor, Palestinian and Hill Prince. She ran second to Hill Prince in the Sunset Handicap. She almost won the Santa Anita Handicap in 1951 but was not quite able to give Moonrush seven pounds on the scale and lost by a neck.

TWO LEA, a champion at three and four, is remembered for setting a brisk pace in the 1950 Santa Anita Handicap before finishing third behind Noor and Citation. Two Lea must have been better than Next Move because she defeated Moonrush while spotting him ten pounds on the scale. She beat some fine females in her career, but she was unable to handle a stablemate, the good colt Ponder, in the Santa Anita Maturity.

1940 – 1945

100.0	Count Fleet
97.8	Twilight Tear (f.)
97.6	Shut Out
	Devil Diver
97.4	Our Boots
	Whirlaway
	Alsab
97.2	Market Wise
96.4	Pensive
96.2	Stir Up
	Attention
	Bimelech
96.0	Lucky Draw
	Challedon
	War Relic
	Mioland
95.8	By Jimminy
	Blue Swords
	Sun Again
	Requested
	Hoop Jr.
95.6	War Jeep
	Stymie
	Ocean Wave

	Valdina Orphan
95.4	Pot o' Luck
	Slide Rule
	With Regards
95.2	Darby Dieppe
	Eurasian
	Rounders
	Marriage
	Thumbs Up
	Apache
	Riverland
	Fenelon
	Isolater
	Hash
95.0	Air Sailor
	First Fiddle
	Mar-Kell (f.)
	Pictor
	Your Chance
94.8	Jeep
	Princequillo
	Roman
	Andy K.
94.6	Gallorette (f.)

1945 – 1950

100.8	Citation
97.8	Busher (f.)
97.6	Armed
97.4	Assault
97.0	Noor
96.8	Capot
96.6	Coaltown
96.0	Lucky Draw
	Seven Hearts
	My Request
95.8	Polynesian
	Lord Boswell
	Your Host
	Vulcan's Forge
95.6	Stymie
	Pavot
	Spy Song
	Hampden
	With Pleasure
	Ponder
95.4	Natchez
	Jet Pilot
	Greek Ship
	Palestinian

	Two Lea (f.)
95.2	Rico Monte
	Phalanx
	Fervent
	Better Self
	Old Rockport
	Next Move (f.)
95.0	Talon
	Faultless
	First Fiddle
	Air Sailor
	Conniver (f.)
	Olympia
	Bewitch (f.)
94.8	First Flight (f.)
	On Trust
	But Why Not (f.)
	Fighting Step
	Miss Request (f.)
94.6	I Will
	Cosmic Bomb
	Gallorette (f.)
	Honeymoon (f.)
94.4	Double Jay

1950 – 1960

HILL PRINCE was voted champion at ages two, three and four, which is very unusual for a horse who was not a great one like Seattle Slew or Affirmed. In those days, there were two actual races in which horses carried their Experimental Handicap weights, and Hill Prince won the first one. He was not, hower, the Experimental highweight. That honor went to Middleground, winner in the 1950 Kentucky Derby. Hill Prince defeated Middleground three times – in the Wood, the Withers and the Preakness.

COUNTERPOINT defeated Hill Prince twice – in the 1951 Jockey Club Gold Cup and the Empire City Gold Cup. A true distance horse, he won all four of his starts at a mile and a half or longer. Counterpoint won with 130 pounds when he was three. A late bloomer, he won seven of his last eight races.

ONE COUNT in 1952 was somewhat like Counterpoint. He too was late-developing, and they won some of the same distance races, including the Belmont. Both horses were sons of Count Fleet, and both champions lost more races than they won. One Count nailed down his Horse of the Year honors by defeating his archrival Mark-Ye-Well in the Jockey Club Gold Cup.

REAL DELIGHT was one of the best fillies of the decade. In 1952 she won eleven out of twelve races, losing by a head to the crack male sprinter White Skies. She never lost to another filly. One of her greatest victories came in the Modesty Handicap. In this race, she gave eighteen pounds and a drubbing to the older Sickle's Image, who was a future champion herself. Real Delight was a winner of the original Triple Tiara, consisting of the Kentucky Oaks, the Black-Eyed Susan and the Coaching Club American Oaks.

TOM FOOL was the first of four great horses to race in the fifties. His Horse-of the-Year season, 1953, was one for the ages. He went undefeated in ten races in the tough handicap division, a feat considered an impossibility at that time. Since then, Spectacular Bid and Cigar have achieved this. Tom Fool also captured the Handicap Triple Crown, which had not been won in forty years. To accomplish this, he had to win the Brooklyn Handicap under 136 pounds. In his career, Tom Fool won twenty-one of thirty starts. He hardly ever traveled. Only twice did he venture outside of New York. Tom Fool was the broodmare sire of Foolish Pleasure.

NATIVE DANCER was the greatest horse of the fifties and one of the very greatest of all time. He won twenty-one of twenty-two starts, which is even better than Man o' War's record. He may have been the best two-year-old of the century, a winner of all nine of his starts in 1952. That year he equaled a world record and also set a new earnings record for juveniles. In 1953 he won everything except the Kentucky Derby, which he lost by a head after being roughed up at the start and forced wide.

At four, Native Dancer was voted Horse of the Year despite only three races. He won all three, carrying 137 pounds in his last start. One poll had named him Horse of the Year at two as well. Native Dancer was a very influential sire. He fathered Raise a Native, who was the sire of Majestic Prince and Alydar and the grandsire of Affirmed. Native Dancer was also the broodmare sire of Northern Dancer and Ruffian.

HIGH GUN was voted a champion at both three and four, but he was not exactly dominant in either year. He was not the most talented sophomore of 1954, and there was even some doubt as to whether he was best in 1955. High Gun ran twice at four against Helioscope and lost both times. In the Suburban, Helioscope won under 128 pounds, with High Gun second under 133. In the Monmouth Handicap Helioscope won under 131 pounds, with High Gun second under 135. High Gun did win under 132, spotting Paper Tiger twenty-five pounds. In 1956, the good handicapper Dedicate lost to Paper Tiger, unable to concede him fourteen pounds.

ERRARD KING was the best three-year-old of 1954, but he did not win the title because he did not compete in any long-distance races.

He scored in the Arlington Classic by 2 ½ lengths with Helioscope second and High Gun third, just a nose farther back. Errard King next captured the American Derby. High Gun, who had won the Belmont, finished second, and Hasty Road, who had won the Preakness, came in third. Kentucky Derby winner Determine unfortunately did not compete in these races.

SARATOGA was the third best three-year-old of 1955, but never attracted much attention because Nashua and Swaps were so superb. In a different year he might have been a champion. He fought so hard in the Preakness that he pushed Nashua to a track-record performance. Nashua won by only one length. Left seven lengths farther back was Traffic Judge, a horse who beat Dedicate five times. These were all very good runners, members of an exceptional crop that also included Bardstown, Summer Tan and Sailor.

NASHUA was Horse of the Year in 1955 on the strength of his historic match race victory, by a decisive six and a half lengths, over archrival Swaps, who had beaten him in the Kentucky Derby. Both were great horses. Nashua won the Preakness and Belmont, races in which Swaps did not compete. He won the Jockey Club Gold Cup twice, setting a new American record for two miles in 1956. His best race that year may have been the Suburban, which he won while conceding seventeen pounds to as good a horse as Dedicate, who became a champion in 1957. Nashua became the new world's leading money winner in 1956, surpassing Citation. He won twenty-two of thirty starts. Shuvee was his daughter.

One reason SWAPS and Nashua only met twice was that Swaps was a California horse, the best one ever bred in that state. He never raced in New York, where Nashua was based. Swaps won nineteen of twenty-five races and was Horse of the Year in 1956. That year he posted five world records, usually under 130 pounds. Swaps also set one world mark in 1955. That year, he defeated another Kentucky Derby winner, Determine. Unlike Man o' War, Swaps did not win by many lengths in any of his record races, indicating that other horses of his day were running surprisingly fast. He sired two top stars of the sixties, the stayer Chateaugay and the sprinter Affectionately.

BOLD RULER is held in high esteem today, but those who

remember the fifties will recall that he was not considered a great horse at the time he was running. But he was close to it. For example, he won the Ben Franklin by twelve lengths while carrying 136 pounds when he was only three. He was part of a mighty triumvirate of outstanding horses of the same age, the others being Gallant Man and Round Table. These three titans met in the 1957 Trenton Handicap in a showdown to decide the championship. Bold Ruler won and snagged the Horse of the Year title.

The sophomores of 1957 were so good that many track records were posted that year. Bold Ruler had four of them. The Trenton proved that he was better than Round Table, but you could deduce that anyway from their races against Clem in 1958. Bold Ruler beat Clem in the Suburban while spotting him twenty-five pounds. Round Table lost to Clem in the United Nations while conceding seventeen pounds. Bold Ruler was one of the greatest sires of all time. He was the sire of Secretariat, the grandsire of Spectacular Bid, and the great-grandsire of Seattle Slew. He won twenty-three of thirty-three races.

GALLANT MAN was almost as good as Bold Ruler. In fact, he came out ahead in half of their eight confrontations. His successes are a bit suspect, however. He outfooted his rival in the Kentucky Derby and the Woodward – both races in which neither horse ran as well as he should have. He won the Belmont by eight lengths in American-record time, the greatest performance of his career. However, that race was at a marathon distance that Bold Ruler couldn't handle.

Gallant Man also won the Metropolitan, in which the weights were not fair. Three of Bold Ruler's four successes seem valid: the Wood, the Trenton and the Carter. Gallant Man raced three times against Round Table and did better every time. In 1958 he won at 1 5/8 miles under 132 pounds. He was the sire of Gallant Bloom and the broodmare sire of Genuine Risk.

ROUND TABLE was never able to handle Gallant Man and was manifestly not as good as Bold Ruler. Yet he was a very exceptional racer, a Horse of the Year in 1958, a handicap champion in 1959, and a world's leading money winner. He made sixty-six starts in just four years and won forty-three races – more than Kelso, who raced a lot longer. He held fifteen track records including one world mark and two

American records under 132 pounds. He thus ran in record time every third time he won. He went through one period (1957-58) in which he won nineteen out of twenty races, just like Citation in 1948. He was the best grass horse of the century, winning fourteen of sixteen turf races under as much as 136 pounds.

GEN DUKE was yet another outstanding horse from the same crop, one who is seldom mentioned anymore because his career was quite short. He ran against Bold Ruler four times in Florida. In the Bahamas Stakes, Bold Ruler won easily while conceding twelve pounds to the Calumet Farm star. In the Everglades, Gen. Duke won by just a head, but that result has no meaning because the weight spread was again twelve pounds. In the Flamingo, they met at equal weights, and Bold Ruler won by a neck in track-record time.

In the Florida Derby, Gen. Duke won by 1 ½ lengths. We think this result might have been a fluke caused by the fact that Gen. Duke had had a previous race over the strip and Bold Ruler had not. Regardless, the race shows that Gen. Duke was an exceptional horse because the time was a world record. Earlier in 1957, Gen. Duke had lost by six lengths to Gallant Man.

The remaining fifties horses were not as good as those profiled above, but they were important performers deserving of recognition. SWOON'S SON was a year older than the stars described above, but he ran a long time, from 1955 through 1958. He was at one time the fourth leading money winner in American history, trailing only Round Table, Nashua and Citation. He won thirty of fifty-one starts, which is slightly better than the record of Equipoise. Swoon's Son was a big star of the Midwest and rarely ran anywhere else. His greatest victory was the 1958 Equipoise Mile in which he defeated Bardstown. He lost twice to Round Table.

Bred in the purple, TIM TAM was the son of Tom Fool and Two Lea and was voted champion three-year-old of 1958. He won ten of fourteen starts, which might sound better than it should because he ran in a very weak year. During the fifties, the good crops were three in the odd-numbered years, and the not-so-good crops in the even-numbered years. Tim Tam won both the Kentucky Derby and the Preakness, beating pedestrian fields. He was the only fifties horse to win both races. Sadly, his Triple Crown hopes were dashed in the Belmont when he broke his leg. There is nothing in Tim Tam's record that shouts Triple Crown. We suspect he would have lost the Belmont anyway. Only really exceptional horses win the Triple Crown. You have to be something more than just the best horse.

BUG BRUSH was the most gifted filly of the fifties, but she couldn't run on the sandy eastern tracks. There have been wonderful eastern horses who couldn't perform in the west. Such superstars as Kelso and Seattle Slew failed in California, but they were sent packing in a hurry as soon as it became clear that they didn't like it there. Why Bug Brush was kept in the east, after it became obvious that she couldn't handle the tracks there, is one of the great mysteries of modern racing.

In California, Bug Brush was a sensation. Her greatest victory was over the immensely talented Hillsdale in the 1959 San Antonio Handicap. The time was a world record. She whipped competent males in the Inglewood Handicap, and nearly beat them a third time in the San Bernardino Handicap. Against her own sex in California, she was invincible.

HILLSDALE, like Bug Brush a four-year-old in 1959, had a superlative record that year. He had ten wins and three seconds in thirteen starts, including a streak of seven consecutive victories. His greatest triumph may have been the Aqueduct Handicap. He shouldered 132 pounds and defeated future champion Bald Eagle, who carried only 122. Had he managed to win the Woodward Stakes, Hillsdale would have been Horse of the Year and champion older horse. However, he lost the race by a head and did not win either award.

SWORD DANCER was champion three-year-old and Horse of the Year in 1959, mostly on the strength of his victory over Hillsdale and Round Table in the climactic Woodward Stakes. Sword Dancer outran Round Table in the Jockey Club Gold Cup as well, but it seems impossible to believe that the California superstar could have been at his best in the fall of 1959. Perhaps he was just worn out from four years of hard racing. Sword Dancer won the Belmont Stakes and lost a roughly run Kentucky Derby by a nose. In 1960, he was one of the better racers in America, but not the same exceptional horse he had been in 1959. Sword Dancer was the sire of the great Damascus.

1950 – 1955

100.8	Native Dancer
99.6	Tom Fool
97.2	Counterpoint
97.0	Noor
	Hill Prince
96.6	Middleground
96.4	Errard King
	One Count
96.2	Determine
	Helioscope
	High Gun
	Traffic Judge
	Mark-Ye-Well
96.0	Hasty Road
	Social Outcast
	Crafty Admiral
	Spartan Valor
95.8	Rejected
	Hall of Fame
	Battlefield
95.6	Imbros
	White Skies
	Alerted
	Turn-to

95.4	Dark Star
	Straight Face
	Berseem
	Sailor
	Real Delight (f.)
	Royal Vale
	Greek Ship
	Correlation
95.2	Money Broker
	Find
	Hasseyampa
95.0	Jamie K.
	Invigorator
	Fisherman
94.8	Royal Bay Gem
94.6	Bed o' Roses (f.)
94.4	Busanda (f.)

1955 – 1960

99.6	Swaps
	Nashua
98.8	Bold Ruler
98.6	Gallant Man
98.4	Round Table
98.2	Gen. Duke
96.8	Sword Dancer
	Bug Brush (f.)
96.6	Hillsdale
96.4	Swoon's Son
	Vertex
	Saratoga
96.2	Bardstown
	Bald Eagle
	High Gun
	Traffic Judge
96.0	Tomy Lee
	Iron Liege
	Summer Tan
	Dedicate
95.8	Intentionally
	First Landing
	Nance's Lad
	Inside Tract

95.6	Restless Wind
	Needles
	Prince John
	Misty Morn (f.)
	Tim Tam
	Terrang
	Promised Land
	Reneged
95.4	Amerigo
	Berlo (f.)
	Fabius
	Career Boy
	Blue Sparkler (f.)
	Sailor
	Berseem
	Jewel's Reward
	Clem
	Federal Hill
95.2	Bagdad
	Royal Native (f.)
	Find
	Alidon
	Mister Gus
	Bobby Brocato
	Porterhouse
	Nadir
95.0	Royal Orbit
	Silver Spoon (f.)
94.0	Silky Sullivan

1960 – 1970

CARRY BACK was one of the high money-winning horses of the sixties, a millionaire at a time when that was still rare. With his thrilling stretch runs and his plebeian pedigree, he became one of the decade's most popular horses. Carry Back was a major star for four years, but he won only one title – champion three-year-old of 1961. After winning the Kentucky Derby and Preakness, he was a heavy favorite to take the Belmont because his closing style was expected to benefit him at the longer distance. He finished seventh, and it eventually became clear that he was not a distance horse at all. He made six attempts to go beyond ten furlongs, and he lost every race. Carry Back was not too successful at beating horses of other ages. He finished behind Ridan, Never Bend and Intentionally.

PROVE IT never won a title because he was the same age as perpetual champion Kelso, but he was a very good handicap horse who beat the talented T. V. Lark seven times. He ran mostly in California and occasionally in Illinois, where he held two track records at Arlington Park under 130 and 131 pounds. We rate Prove It the second best horse owned by Rex Ellsworth, ranking him between the incomparable Swaps and Preakness winner Candy Spots.

JAIPUR, champion sophomore of 1962, was an exciting horse because he was in a lot of close races, battling valiantly all the way to the wire. After losing two close ones in 1961, he was undefeated in such contests in 1962. He lost the Jersey Derby by a nose, but the winner was disqualified. He then captured the Belmont by a nose. The 1962 Travers was so thrilling that some experts considered it the greatest spectacle since the 1950 San Juan Capistrano. Jaipur defeated archrival Ridan by a nose. Kelso vanquished him in the Woodward Stakes, and some say this race broke his heart because he never won again.

KELSO was one of the three or four greatest American horses of the twentieth century. He was voted Horse of the Year for five consecutive seasons, 1960-1964, a feat never duplicated either before or since. He won thirty-nine races and was the world's leading money winner for fifteen years. Like Tom Fool eight years earlier, Kelso swept the rarely won Handicap Triple Crown, annexing the Brooklyn under 136 pounds. His favorite race was the two-mile Jockey Club Gold Cup, which he won five times in a row. In 1964 he set a new American record in the race, breaking his own record. After losing the Washington D. C. International three times, the persistent Kelso finally won it in 1964, posting a new American record.

For years, Kelso had been winning almost everything without much of an argument from other horses. That changed at the end of 1963 when MONGO defeated Kelso in the Washington D. C. International. Then, in 1964, GUN BOW emerged as a second threat to Kelso's supremacy. All three horses clashed in the Monmouth Handicap. Mongo (127 pounds) won by a neck. Kelso (130) was second, and Gun Bow (124) was third.

Mongo whipped Gun Bow three times: the Monmouth, the J. B. Campbell Memorial and the Grey Lag Handicap. Gun Bow beat Mongo once, in the Whitney. Gun Bow beat Kelso by a diminishing nose in the Woodward Stakes, but Kelso defeated Gun Bow three times: in the Monmouth, the Aqueduct Stakes and the Washington D. C. International, the victory that finally settled the Horse of the Year issue in favor of Kelso. Gun Bow's broodmare sire was War Admiral, and Kelso's broodmare sire was Count Fleet.

NORTHERN DANCER in 1964 was named champion three-year-old in America and Horse of the Year in Canada. A consistent colt, he won fourteen of eighteen starts, eight of which took place in his native Canada. Northern Dancer set a new track record in the Kentucky Derby. He then added the Preakness to his resume, but he was unable to stay the Belmont distance and finished third. He made one more start, easily winning the Queen's Plate. Northern Dancer never faced older horses, but it seems unlikely he would have had much success against

Kelso, Mongo or Gun Bow. He became one of the great sires, but he seemed to have better luck in Europe than here.

ROMAN BROTHER was named 1965 Horse of the Year in one poll. He was nowhere near as good as Kelso, but that superhorse, then eight, was too old to maintain a heavy schedule anymore. Roman Brother won just five of fourteen starts in 1965, and two of his victories were allowance races. He was only the fourth best horse in his crop, outranked by Northern Dancer, Quadrangle and Pia Star. You could even place him fifth if you think Hill Rise was better. Roman Brother always beat Hill Rise in New York, but never in other states. We consider them equal. Roman Brother earned more than $940,000, a tidy sum to make from just forty-two starts.

TOSMAH was one of the best fillies of the sixties. She won championships at two and three, but she was still very good at four and five. She was evidently better than Cicada, another multiple champion. Cicada was unable to give Old Hat nine pounds in the 1963 Suwannee River Handicap, but Tosmah beat Old Hat in the 1964 Maskette Handicap while spotting her eleven pounds on the scale. Old Hat was a good mare, a champion twice. In 1965 Tosmah beat champion sprinter Affectionately in the one-mile Maskette. She almost equaled a world record in the 1966 Equipoise Mile. Tosmah beat males four times. Her sire was Tim Tam.

NATIVE DIVER was a popular California star who raced for seven years, making eighty-one starts. In the 1965 San Carlos Handicap, he defeated Preakness winner Candy Spots. He also equaled a world record that year in the Los Angeles Handicap. He would have been a better choice for Horse of the Year than Roman Brother, but in those days there was prejudice against horses who didn't race in the east. Native Diver had tremendous speed, but he could carry it a long way. He won the Hollywood Gold Cup three years in a row. He won under 133 pounds when he was eight.

LUCKY DEBONAIR was a horse with a lot of ability, but he was very fragile and couldn't put in a full season of work. As a result, he never won a title. In 1965 he prepped for the Kentucky Derby with wins in the Santa Anita Derby and Blues Grass Stakes. He then won the Kentucky Derby, beating some good horses like Tom Rolfe and

Bold Lad. In 1966 he became the first Derby winner to capture the Santa Anita Handicap, defeating Native Diver, Hill Rise and other good runners.

Great horses sometimes come in bunches, and there were three of them that raced in 1966 and 1967. The oldest of these was the fantastic BUCKPASSER, who was three in 1966. He won thirteen of fourteen races that year and was unanimously named Horse of the Year. He also was voted champion of his division at two and four. Altogether he won twenty-five of thirty-one races, including fifteen in a row. He was the first horse to become a millionaire when he was only three. Buckpasser set a world record in the Arlington Classic. He won under 133 pounds at four. His sire was Tom Fool, and his broodmare sire was War Admiral. He himself was the broodmare sire of Easy Goer and Slew o' Gold.

DAMASCUS and DR. FAGER were bitter archrivals, one year younger than Buckpasser. These two great ones met twice in 1967 and twice in 1968. In the Gotham Stakes, Dr. Fager was the victor, but he did not set the pace the way he usually did. He came from behind and passed Damascus in the stretch.

The Woodward Stakes, billed as the "Race of the Decade," was exactly that. The two valiant gladiators would be challenged by Buckpasser! Damascus and Buckpasser each ran coupled with a "rabbit" who was supposed to tire out the speed-crazy Dr. Fager. The strategy worked, and Damascus turned the race into a complete rout, trouncing Buckpasser by ten lengths. This smashing victory assured Damascus the Horse of the Year award.

The 1968 Suburban may have been the most authentic meeting of the two titans. The weights were almost the same, and no rabbits were entered. Dr. Fager defeated Damascus by five lengths. The final showdown was the Brooklyn, but this time the weights were not fair. Damascus (130 pounds) defeated Dr. Fager (135) by 2 ½ lengths. It was the only loss Dr. Fager suffered in 1968, enabling him to win the Horse of the Year award. He also was honored as Best Handicapper, Best Sprinter and Best Grass Horse – an unprecedented sweep!

Both these great horses turned in some eye-popping, mind-boggling performances. In the 1967 Travers, Damascus romped home by 22 lengths! In the 1968 Washington Park Handicap, Dr. Fager won by ten lengths in world-record time under 134 pounds. His record stood for twenty-nine years. In the United Nations Handicap, Dr. Fager, with no grass experience, defeated Fort Marcy, who was a grass champion himself, while spotting him sixteen pounds! In the Vosburgh Handicap, Dr. Fager set a track record while lugging 139 pounds. He and Damascus carried on the best rivalry since Nashua and Swaps twelve years earlier.

STAGE DOOR JOHNNY was the champion three-year-old of 1968. He made just six starts that year, winning his last five in a row. Stage Door Johnny was by Prince John, a stamina influence in a pedigree. Fittingly, his most important victory was the Belmont Stakes, in which he vanquished Forward Pass, the Kentucky Derby and Preakness winner. The time was quite fast for that era–just a few ticks slower than Gallant Man's record. The third horse was left twelve lengths behind the dueling favorites. In his last start, the Dwyer, Stage Door Johnny toted 129 pounds – one pound more than Damascus carried in his Dwyer.

GAMELY, a daughter of Bold Ruler, won three titles between 1967 and 1969. In her best year, 1968, she did very well against males. She won the Inglewood and finished second to Dr. Fager in the Californian. In both these races she outran the capable colt Rising Market. Moreover, she whipped her stablemate Princessnesian three times, and that filly won the Hollywood Gold Cup. Gamely carried the heavy burden of 131 pounds when she won the Vanity Handicap.

GALLANT BLOOM in 1969 proved she was the decade's best filly. She won all eight of her starts that year. In her career she won sixteen of twenty-two races. She defeated older champion Gamely by seven lengths in the Matchmaker. This is important because she had no credentials against males, but Gamely did, suggesting that Gallant Bloom could have handled males at fair weights very well. Another famous filly that Gallant Bloom beat was Shuvee, winner of the Triple Tiara that year. Gallant Bloom romped home in the Monmouth Oaks by twelve lengths.

MAJESTIC PRINCE in 1969 tried to accomplish what Seattle Slew did eight years later: he sought to become an undefeated Triple Crown winner. A California horse trained by Johnny Longden, Majestic

Prince swept his first seven races in a row, his most important win being the Santa Anita Derby. He went into the Kentucky Derby with his perfect record and – presto! – he won the Derby by a neck over archrival ART AND LETTERS. He tallied once again in the Preakness, this time by a head over his rival. Now he was nine-for-nine! Unfortunately, Arts and Letters crushed our hero by more than five lengths in the Belmont.

Strenuous racing takes a heavy toll on some horses. Majestic Prince was all worn out by then. He never raced again. Longden didn't even want to start him in the Belmont, but the owner insisted. With Majestic Prince gone from the stage, and the once-formidable Top Knight completely off form, Arts and Letters had an easy time of it, sweeping four big stakes in a row. In the Jockey Club Gold Cup, he demolished the top older horse, Nodouble, by fourteen lengths. Arts and Letters won the Horse of the Year title on the basis of this late-season surge. Majestic Prince sired the successful grass horse Majestic Light.

TA WEE was the best female sprinter since Pan Zareta. She didn't have a long career like that indestructible mare, but she was more consistent, winning fifteen of twenty-one starts. Ta Wee was voted champion sprinter twice, in 1969 and 1970. She managed a slightly better record than Myrtlewood's, even though she was carrying higher weights. Ta Wee beat Rising Market, as Gamely had done. She also beat Shuvee. The most weight she won with was 142 pounds. Ta Wee was certainly bred for speed! Her sire was Intentionally, a sprint champion himself, and she had the same dam as lightning-fast Dr Fager. Both Intentionally and Dr. Fager set world records for a mile.

1960 – 1965

100.8	Kelso
97.2	Mongo
97.0	Gun Bow
96.4	Prove It
96.2	Jaipur
	Sir Gaylord
	Bald Eagle
	T. V. Lark
	Northern Dancer
	Native Diver
	Beau Purple
96.0	Ridan
	Bally Ache
	Raise a Native
	Pia Star
	Quadrangle
	Candy Spots
	Chateaugay
	The Axe II
95.8	Hail to Reason
	Carry Back
	Intentionally
	Venetian Way
	Roman Brother

	Hill Rise
	Never Bend
95.6	Dapper Dan
	Bold Lad
	Globemaster
	Crozier
	Victoria Park
	Tompion
	Crimson Satan
95.4	Royal Gunner
	George Royal
	Tosmah (f.)
	Four-and-Twenty
	Yorky
	Celtic Ash
95.2	Native Charger
	Hail to All
	Affectionately (f.)
	Cicada (f.)
	Olden Times
	Beau Prince
	Ambiopoise
	Divine Comedy
95.0	Malicious
	Admiral's Voyage
94.6	Old Hat (f.)

1965 – 1970

100.0	Dr. Fager
99.8	Damascus
99.6	Buckpasser
96.8	Majestic Prince
	Top Knight
96.6	Arts and Letters
96.4	Stage Door Johnny
	Dike
	Lucky Debonair
	Pretense
96.2	Forward Pass
	Al Hattab
	Tom Rolfe
	Native Diver
96.0	Exclusive Native
	Out of the Way
	Dancer's Image
	Ack Ack
	Quadrangle
95.8	Iron Ruler
	Nodouble
	In Reality
	Graustark
	Personality

95.6	Fort Marcy
	Proud Clarion
	Kauai King
	Fast Hilarious
	Gallant Bloom (f.)
95.4	Royal Gunner
	Handsome Boy
	Bold Hour
	Impressive
	Ta Wee (f.)
	Night Invader
	Gamely (f.)
	Dark Mirage (f.)
95.2	Buffle
	Amberoid
	Successor
	Mr. Right
	Verbatim
	Rising Market
	Princessnesian (f.)
95.0	Malicious
	Quicken Tree
	Amerigo Lady (f.)
	Shuvee (f.)
94.8	Terry's Secret
94.6	Bold Bidder
93.2	Moccasin (f.)

1970 – 1980

FORT MARCY was Horse of the Year in 1970 and a grass champion twice, in 1970 and 1967. The best horse he ever beat was Damascus, but that result only proved that Damascus didn't like grass. Good horses that Fort Marcy beat include Hawaii, Quicken Tree, Fiddle Isle and Drumtop. Alas, he also lost to each of these horses – but at least it shows that he could run in good company. It's easier to identify what horses he was worse than than what horses he was better than. The Gulfstream Park Handicap shows that he was not as good as Nodouble, and the Hollywood Invitational Turf shows that he was not as good as Cougar II. Fort Marcy won just twenty-one of seventy-five races. That's really not too good, but it was enough to make him a millionaire in an era when that was still unusual.

ACK ACK was Horse of the Year in 1971. All of his starts were in California, where he won the Hollywood Gold Cup under 134 pounds. When he ran in the east in 1969, however, he was not the best. He was sixth best in his crop, outranked by Majestic Prince, Top Knight, Arts and Letters, Dike and Al Hattab. You can see the difference in the quality of his opponents by looking at his batting averages. He won eighty-five percent of his starts out west, but just fifty-seven percent of his starts in the east. The best horse he beat was Cougar II. We may also infer that he was better than Nodouble. In the American Handicap, he gave eleven pounds and a thumping to Figonero. In the Californian, Nodouble was unable to spot Figonero six pounds.

RIVA RIDGE and KEY TO THE MINT were embittered enemies for three years. At two, Riva was the champion and beat Key twice. At three, Key was the champion, outrunning Riva three out of four meetings. At four, Riva was the champion, defeating Key in two of three confrontations. Seven of these nine races are inconclusive – races in which at least one, or occasionally both, failed to run his race.

The two events we consider most relevant are the 1972 Woodward, won by Key with Riva fourth, and the 1973 Brooklyn, won by Riva with Key fourth. The latter race was a world-record performance by Riva Ridge. Thus, the two stars appeared to be almost the same in ability. Key to the Mint did better in the stud. He was a half-brother of Fort Marcy.

PROVE OUT was the only horse besides the lightly raced Sham who beat both Secretariat and Forego. When Sham did it in the Wood (Secretariat) and in the Kentucky Derby (Forego), he did not win either race – but the amazing Prove Out won both of his. In August 1973, having much the best of the weights, he outran Forego. About a month later, at fair weights, he defeated Secretariat! Prove Out, of course, was not better than Secretariat. The latter just didn't have it that day – he didn't fire.

In the Jockey Club Gold Cup in October, Prove Out showed that he really was quite a good horse at that time. In this race he took on Riva Ridge – and he wiped him out by twenty-three lengths! Riva was prominent early and had every chance to win, but he just couldn't stay with Prove Out after the two of them had pulled sixteen lengths ahead of the field, battling it out until one of them cracked. Prove Out really did prove out!

SECRETARIAT was truly "great among the greats" in the sense that he was the finest horse of the seventies, a decade that produced four other great males, more than any other decade. He ran for only two seasons and was Horse of the Year both times, in 1972 and 1973. He was such a celebrity that he appeared on the cover of national news magazines like Time and Newsweek. Man o' War had done that back in the twenties.

Secretariat became the first Triple Crown winner in twenty-five years. There actually had been only seven horses since 1948 who even had a chance at the crown. All had failed. Secretariat began his quest by becoming the first horse ever to win the Kentucky Derby in less than two minutes. In the Preakness, he erupted with such a powerful move that people still remember it. In the Belmont, he stunned onlookers by sprinting the entire mile and a half! His time was a new world record, and he won by thirty-one lengths. In September he set another world record when he won the Marlboro Cup over speedy stablemate Riva Ridge. Secretariat also excelled on grass, winning the turf championship too.

DAHLIA was a foreign mare who sometimes raced in America. She and Exceller had the same sire. She was racing's first female millionaire and a graded stakes winner in five different countries. Dahlia defeated Grade 1 males three times in America in three different states. In Europe, where the competition on grass in tougher, she whipped Group 1 males five times. For a mare with such immense talent, Dahlia was not too consistent, winning about one-third of her starts. Although not quite the best mare in Europe because of Allez France, she was voted best grass horse of either sex in America in 1974.

DESERT VIXEN was a two-time champion, in both 1973 and 1974. She won the Beldame Stakes, the most coveted prize for fillies and mares on the calendar, in both those years. She beat multiple champion Susan's Girl by nearly twelve lengths in 1973, and she defeated gifted Tizna by eighteen lengths in 1974. Her time in 1973 equaled the American record on dirt. She lost more races than she won, but she was not inconsistent. She was streaky like Assault, once winning eight in a row. One of her greatest races was one that she lost to an obscure male: the 1974 Washington D. C. International. With no experience on grass or over such a long distance, she outran turf champion Dahlia! They were second and third.

RUFFIAN may be most widely remembered for her tragic breakdown in a 1975 match race against one of the best colts in the nation, Foolish Pleasure. He actually was the only serious competition she ever faced. She won her first ten races in a row, a feat aided by the weak fields she encountered. The only other talent in her crop was My Juliet, whom she never met. Opening a career with a fine winning streak does not always indicate greatness. Morvich swept his first twelve races in a row – and then never won again, and his story is not unusual.

We consider Ruffian a great filly, but not as great as some others. We prefer females who proved they could beat Grade 1 males, in some cases just as good as Foolish Pleasure. Ruffian's speed, which one writer called "blinding," seems to have been exaggerated. She held just one track record and no world records. Some fillies have done better than that. Her best fractions are not as good as those of My Juliet, who ran a half in :43. When we compared Ruffian's times with other horses who had the same running style, we discovered that, at nearly all the distances, Bold Forbes ran faster than she.

WAJIMA was the champion sophomore of 1975 – not Foolish Pleasure. The highlight of his career was his upset of the great Forego in the Marlboro Cup. He had slightly the better of the weights, but the fact that he could match strides at all with such a horse is impressive. They met again at scale weights in the Woodward, and Forego retaliated. The Marlboro proved that Wajima was better than Foolish Pleasure. He received four pounds from Forego that day, whereas Foolish Pleasure lost the 1976 Brooklyn to Forego while getting eight pounds.

FOREGO was a Horse of the Year three times – 1974-76 – and a handicap champion four times – 1974-77. He was very versatile. In 1974 he was voted the champion sprinter, but he also won at two miles that year. His greatest, most spectacular victory was the 1976 Marlboro Cup. Under 137 pounds, he came from well behind to score by a head, barely collaring the speedy Honest Pleasure, who toted only 119. This race alone would stamp Forego as a great one, but in such a long career he had other impressive victories as well under staggering weights. He did not accomplish as much as Kelso, but he ran faster. That is to be expected because of the thirteen years' difference in their ages.

CRYSTAL WATER was a very successful California horse who regrettably was not pointed for the Triple Crown. He would have had a decent chance in the Derby and an excellent chance in both the Preakness and the Belmont. In the 1976 El Dorado Handicap, An Act (124 pounds) won, and Crystal Water (125) was second. The speedy Sure Fire ran third under 117. In contrast, in the San Miguel Stakes, Bold Forbes was unable to give Sure Fire six pounds. In 1977 Crystal Water earned more than twice as much money as Forego. He also equaled a world record that year. Crystal Water had a win over Caucasus, the best American horse that Dahlia beat.

SEATTLE SLEW in 1977 became a Triple Crown winner and Horse of the Year. A champion every year he ran, he won fourteen of seventeen starts. He was sort of a part-time hero in that he made fewer starts in three years than Secretariat and Count Fleet had in two. Sir Barton, who ran for three years, raced thirty-one times.

Seattle Slew beat nothing much in 1977, but he proved how great he really was in 1978. In the first meeting ever between Triple Crown winners, Slew defeated the great Affirmed by three lengths in the Marlboro Cup. He was heroic in defeat in the Jockey Club Gold Cup, losing by only a nose after a suicidal pace duel. In the Stuyvesant Handicap, he won under 134 pounds. He became a very great sire, fathering A. P. Indy, Swale and Slew o' Gold. He was the broodmare sire of Cigar.

AFFIRMED was in many respects the most accomplished horse of all time. He was a champion every year he ran, a Horse of the Year twice, a Triple Crown winner, and racing's first multimillionaire. He made twenty-nine starts in three years, winning twenty-two races. Had he not had to face Seattle Slew or Alydar, murderous competition that very few other horses ever encountered, he would have had twenty-six wins and three losses. A winner of fifteen of his first seventeen races, he won fourteen Grade 1 stakes, which is about half his starts. John Henry won a record sixteen Grade 1 races, but that was in eighty-three starts.

People still remember the epic duels between Affirmed and Alydar in the 1978 Triple Crown races. It was the greatest rivalry in racing history because the two gladiators met ten times. Affirmed won seven of these races, and one of his three losses was via disqualification. He only won the Belmont by a head in one of the most thrilling spectacles ever witnessed. Affirmed evidently improved between three and four because in 1979 he defeated the great Spectacular Bid, a better horse than Alydar. This occurred in the Jockey Club Gold Cup, the big, climactic showdown of the year. Another of Affirmed's great victories was the Hollywood Gold Cup, which he won in very fast time under 132 pounds.

ALYDAR was racing's most valiant and heroic loser. He won fourteen of twenty-six starts, the same record as Gallant Man. However, had he not had to face Affirmed, he would have been a Triple Crown winner with twenty wins and six losses, which is almost as good as War Admiral! Alydar won all of his starts in 1978 except for the three losses to Affirmed that year. He took two stakes by thirteen lengths and beat older horses by ten lengths. Even so, we regret to say that he doesn't really have the level of achievement that we expect of a great horse. He did become a very great sire. His offspring include Easy Goer, Alysheba, Turkoman, Althea and Criminal Type.

EXCELLER came here from Europe, where he had won four Group 1 races. He is best remembered for his great victory in the 1978 Jockey Club Gold Cup, in which he came from twenty-two lengths behind to nip Seattle Slew by a nose. This race was actually very fluky in that Slew was all worn out from a killing pace. We think it best to set aside this quirky result and evaluate Exceller on his other races. Seattle Slew defeated him easily in the more normally run Woodward Stakes. In 1977 Exceller, Majestic Light and Johnny D. took turns beating one another in eastern races so that it was impossible to separate them.

In 1978 Exceller went to California, where the competition may have been a little softer than what he had faced in the east. He also may have benefited from a trainer switch to Charlie Whittingham. At any rate, he had his best year in 1978, winning rich stakes on dirt as well as grass. The story of Exceller has a tragic ending. He was murdered in a slaughterhouse in Sweden.

Many people were surprised that Exceller did not win the 1978 grass title. The award went to MAC DIARMIDA instead. He too had had a very good year. He won twelve of thirteen starts on grass. Exceller won four out of six. Exceller won four Grade 1 events. Mac Diarmida won two. However, he lost only one Grade 1, whereas Exceller lost two. It must have been a difficult decision. We think it was correct.

TILLER was an outstanding grass horse who was equally proficient on dirt. In 1978 he finished second in three straight important events. In the Man o' War Stakes, Waya won with Mac Diarmida third. In the Washington D. C. International, Mac Diarmida won by a head over Tiller, with Waya third. In the Turf Classic, Waya won by a nose over Tiller. Thus, the three protagonists were similar in ability. Tiller really scored big in 1979, outrunning Exceller twice, in the Santa Anita Handicap on dirt and the San Juan Capistrano on grass. In the 1980 Sword Dancer Handicap, Tiller defeated multiple grass champion John Henry.

WAYA was a Group 2 winner in France in 1977. Coming to America in 1978, she equaled a world record and competed in the three big stakes mentioned above. She was clearly the best grass female of 1978, but she was cheated out of an award because none was given that year.

In 1979 Waya was the best mare on both grass and dirt. However, in one of the silliest decisions ever made by Eclipse Award voters, they gave the grass accolade to Trillion, who never won a single race in America! The fact that Trillion lost twice to male champion Bowl Game, whom Waya had outrun in the Bowling Green Handicap, shows that Waya was better than Trillion, whom she had beaten in 1978. Waya dragged 131 pounds to victory in the Santa Barbara Handicap on grass. Fortunately for her, she did win the dirt award for best older female.

SPECTACULAR BID was one of the ten greatest horses of the century and the last of the great ones. He became a Horse of the Year in 1980 and a world's leading money winner. He won twenty-six of thirty races, a superlative record. However, it should be remembered that, although there were some quality horses in his crop like Flying Paster and General Assembly, he never had to face really formidable opposition except from Affirmed, to whom he lost. After capturing the Kentucky Derby and Preakness easily, he was upset in the Belmont by Coastal, which ended a twelve-race winning streak. An incident about a safety pin was blamed for his defeat, but it could be that he just wasn't that much of a distance horse.

In 1980 Spectacular Bid won all nine of his starts, which was the first time in twenty-seven years that a horse went undefeated in the handicap division. Like Affirmed, he won under 132 pounds. His people declined an invitation to run packing 136 pounds, which is a shame because he probably could have won under that weight. Tom Fool had done so. Spectacular Bid set a new American record on dirt when he captured the Strub Stakes. The final start of his career, the Woodward Stakes, was a walkover. It's extremely rare in modern racing to have an event in which only one horse "competes." We don't think there has been any walkover since 1980.

1970 – 1975

100.6	Secretariat
98.0	Sham
97.0	Prove Out
96.8	Key to the Mint
	Riva Ridge
96.4	Desert Vixen (f.)
96.2	No Le Hace
	Solar Salute
	Dahlia (f.)
96.0	Freetex
	Hold Your Peace
	Ack Ack
	Quack
95.8	Upper Case
	Personality
	Our Native
	My Gallant
	Cougar II
	Hoist the Flag
95.6	Tentam
	True Knight
	Dust Commander
	Linda's Chief
	Fort Marcy

95.4	Canonero II
	Good Behaving
	King's Bishop
	My Dad George
	Ancient Title
95.2	Bold Reasoning
	Eastern Fleet
	Autobiography
	Corn off the Cob
95.0	Little Current
	Pass Catcher
	Executioner
	Shuvee (f.)
	Silent Screen
94.8	Poker Night (f.)
	Chris Evert (f.)
	Jim French
	Paraje
	High Echelon
94.6	Tizna (f.)
	Bold Reason
	Loud
94.4	Susan's Girl (f.)
	Unconscious
93.6	Mr. Prospector

1975 – 1980

100.4	Seattle Slew
100.2	Affirmed
100.0	Forego
	Spectacular Bid
99.0	Alydar
96.4	An Act
96.2	Wajima
	Dahlia (f.)
	Crystal Water
	Waya (f.)
	Tiller
	Mac Diarmida
96.0	Bold Forbes
	Foolish Pleasure
	Caucasus
	King Pellinore
	Majestic Light
	Johnny D.
	Exceller
	John Henry
95.8	Ruffian (f.)
	Honest Pleasure
	Crow
	Bowl Game

	Flying Paster
	General Assembly
	Radar Ahead
95.6	Believe it
	Nasty and Bold
	Vigors
	Cascapedia (f.)
	Forceten
	Royal Derby II
	Noble Dance II
	Coastal
	Balzac
95.4	Run Dusty Run
	Junction
	Dava's Friend
	Ancient Title
	My Juliet (f.)
	Messenger of Song
	L'Heureux
	Golden Act
95.2	J.O. Tobin
	Text
	Star de Naskra
	Royal Glint
	Master Derby
	Avatar
	Riot in Paris
95.0	Cox's Ridge
	Sensitive Prince
94.6	Davona Dale (f.)

1980 – 1990

GENUINE RISK in 1980 became just the second filly to win the Kentucky Derby, and the first in sixty-five years. Her victory was a pleasant surprise because she had just lost the Wood Memorial to Plugged Nickle. She went on to run second to Codex in the Preakness and second to Temperence Hill in the Belmont. Never before had a filly ever done so well in the spring classics, nor did it ever happen again. In the Ruffian Handicap she beat older females. She lost the Maskette to the talented Bold 'n Determined, but no one held it against her, and she was voted the champion away.

CONQUISTADOR CIELO was ultimately selected 1982 Horse of the Year in what was initially a three-way tie with Landaluce and Lemhi Gold. He actually wrapped up the three-year-old title in less than a week, setting a track record in the Metropolitan Mile on May 31 and then running off with the Belmont by fourteen lengths on June 5. A horse with a lot of early speed, he led all the way in winning his prep for the Travers. Alas, things did not go well for him in the Travers. He tried to set the pace as usual, but a stubborn Aloma's Ruler stayed with him and kept slugging it out until both horses were exhausted. Aloma's Ruler finished second, and Conquistador Cielo had to settle for third. This race is reminiscent of the 1949 Sysonby Mile, proving once again that class is more important than speed.

ALL ALONG in 1983 became the first foreign Horse of the Year. This French filly was a surprise winner of the Arc de Triomphe, the most prestigious race in Europe. She then came to North America and swept three straight Grade I events, one of them in Canada. She thus became Horse of the Year having had only two starts in the United States! All Along did not win in 1984, but she was a close second in the Breeders' Cup Turf and ran third in the Arc. Round Table was her grandsire.

JOHN HENRY became America's all-time leading money winner, a four-time grass champion, and a Horse of Year twice, the second time at the unprecedented age of nine. His sixteen Grade I victories were a twentieth century record. His best year was 1981, the only year he was a champion on dirt as well as on grass. He was six at that time. In 1984 he was honored on the basis of his prowess on grass. He lost on dirt to such good horses as Interco and Desert Wine. John Henry won the Arlington Million twice, in 1981 and 1984. He started eighty-three times and won thirty-nine races. A late bloomer, he actually was the same age as Affirmed and Alydar. He equaled a world record in 1980.

SUNNY'S HALO in 1983 was the best horse in what turned out to be a superior crop of three-year-olds. A Canadian star, he won the Kentucky Derby over Desert Wine, Caveat and Slew o' Gold – all fine horses. We actually think he was more talented than Canada's biggest star, Northern Dancer. His greatest victory came in the Super Derby, which he won by ten lengths over Travers winner Play Fellow.

SLEW O' GOLD was named champion twice, in 1983 and 1984. At three, he was only the fifth best horse in his crop, outranked by Sunny's Halo, Play Fellow, Desert Wine and Caveat. You can tell that his fourth-place finish in the Kentucky Derby was a valid gauge of his ability because Caveat, who outran him in the Derby, defeated him again in the Belmont. Moreover, Play Fellow, who had bested Desert Wine in the Blue Grass, whipped Slew o' Gold in the Travers.

Bates Motel, the older champion in 1983, was defeated by Slew o' Gold in the Woodward because he was not as good as the leading three-year-olds. Slew o' Gold, who won just five of twelve races in 1983, had a better year in 1984, winning all of his starts except the roughly run Breeders' Cup Classic. The most talented horse that Slew o' Gold beat in 1984 was Track Barron, who won some important races in 1985.

ALTHEA was a champion at two and still very good at three. As a juvenile she beat the boys twice, in the Hollywood Juvenile and the Del Mar Futurity, races that fillies seldom enter. In the 1984 Arkansas Derby at three, she blazed to a new track record, trouncing At the Threshold and Gate Dancer, males who were prominent in the

Kentucky Derby finish. Althea herself ran in the Derby but couldn't handle the distance and dropped far back. This grueling race completely wiped her out permanently.

It seems such a pity that Althea didn't skip the Derby and point for the Preakness. The shorter distance would have been better for her, she would have been a fresh horse going against weary Derby survivors, and she had already beaten Gate Dancer, who won the Preakness. Althea was a lot more talented than her stablemate Life's Magic, even though the latter was ultimately more successful.

SPEND A BUCK was a Horse of the Year at three in 1985. His grandsire was Buckpasser. He was not expected to win the Kentucky Derby because it was anticipated that he would be in a pace war with the speedy Eternal Prince. However, that horse didn't break well, leaving our hero on the lead by himself. He pulled steadily away from his field and won easily in very fast time. However, he skipped both the Preakness and Belmont, to the dismay of many racing fans.

Garden State was offering a $2 million bonus prize if Spend a Buck could win the Jersey Derby, and his owners decided to go after the money. Spend a Buck did win the race and the bonus, edging Creme Fraiche, who went on to succeed in the Belmont. We would have liked to see Spend a Buck prove his class a little more. He did win one race against older horses, but they were not the best elders he could have faced. We would have liked to see him compete against Travers and Marlboro Cup winner Chief's Crown, who had not been at his best during the spring classics.

PRECISIONIST earned $3.4 million in five years of racing. In one of the poorest decisions made by Eclipse Award voters, Vanlandingham was chosen champion handicap horse of 1985, an award that should have gone to Precisionist. Vanlandingham merely broke even in two races against Gate Dancer, but Precisionist beat Gate Dancer twice in 1985, in the San Fernando and the Strub. Moreover, he outran Lord at War in the Californian, and Lord at War defeated Gate Dancer in the Santa Anita Handicap.

In the later years, Precisionist continued to be a major player. He was third in the 1986 Breeders Cup Classic behind Skywalker and Turkoman. He beat eventual Horse of the Year Lady's Secret in both the Iselin and the Woodward. Moreover, he defeated Garthorn in the Yankee Valor, and Garthorn vanquished Lady's Secret in the Metropolitan. After taking off all of 1987, Precisionist returned in 1988 to finish second to Forty Niner in the N.Y.R.A. Mile. In 1984 he won the Swaps Stakes by ten lengths, massacring Prince True, another horse who beat Gate Dancer.

Call us old-fashioned, but we like to see the awards go to the best horses. LADY'S SECRET was easily the best female of 1986, but she was clearly not the best horse. In fact, we believer there were at least nine horses better than she that year. In addition to the four already mentioned, we would add Ferdinand, Snow Chief, Danzig Connection, Manila and Theatrical. Among other female Horses of the Year, we think they were all better than Lady's Secret except Moccasin.

Against her own sex, Lady's Secret did plenty. She captured seven Grade I stakes including the Beldame and the Breeders' Cup Distaff. In the only two such races that she lost, the weights were so stacked against her that she had no chance. In 1985 she scored a major coup when she conquered Triple Tiara winner Mom's Command in the Test Stakes. In her whole career she won twenty-five of forty-five starts, a record slightly better than triple champion Cicada, who won twenty-three of forty-two. Lady's Secret, the best daughter of Secretariat, also became America's leading female money winner, supplanting another Horse of the Year, All Along.

Among all the best male stars with their varying levels of achievement in 1986, we believe the one with the best claim to the Horse of the Year title was MANILA. We consider Snow Chief a better horse, but he didn't win after May. Manila, on the other hand, was a major winner as late as November.

Manila finished his season with a six-race winning streak. In his climactic victory in the Breeders' Cup Turf, he defeated all rivals, both male and female, both foreign and domestic. Lady's Secret beat only domestic females in the Distaff. Manila was a champion who twice beat another champion, Theatrical. He won ten of his last eleven starts, including two million-dollar races. However, his times were not as fast as those of John Henry.

Kentucky Derby winner FERDINAND and Preakness winner

SNOW CHIEF were protagonists of the same age who squared off nine times. Snow Chief got the better of his rival six times. Moreover, Ferdinand's three successes included two – the Kentucky Derby and the Santa Anita Handicap – in which Snow Chief pressed the pace too much and tired.

The most thrilling encounter between these valiant rivals was the 1987 Strub Stakes. After a pitched battle down the stretch, Snow Chief won by a nose. Third in this race was Broad Brush, which made this one-two-three finish exactly the same as the 1986 Preakness. Both Snow Chief and Ferdinand won well over three million dollars. Ferdinand's greatest victory was the Breeders' Cup Classic. This win made him 1987 Horse of the Year. Snow Chief won the sophomore championship in 1986.

ALYSHEBA was nosed out by Ferdinand in the 1987 Breeders' Cup Classic, but he was closing fast at the end, and later races indicate that he was a better horse. Alysheba defeated Ferdinand three times in 1988: in the Santa Anita Handicap, the San Bernardino and the Hollywood Gold Cup. That year, following victory in the Breeders' Cup Classic, he became Horse of the Year and America's new leading money winner, surpassing the earnings of John Henry in less than one-third as many starts. In 1987 he won the Kentucky Derby, the Preakness and the three-year-old title.

MIESQUE was a French filly who came to America twice for the Breeders' Cup Mile and won it both times. She was named champion grass female both in 1987 and 1988. Miesque was also a champion in Europe, where she defeated Group I males five times. In the Prix Jacques le Marois, she won with Warning second and Gabina third. This is significant because Blushing John finished behind Gabina in the Prix du Moulin. He then came to America in 1989 and won the handicap title. Thus, Miesque was a champion who was quite a bit better than another champion. She won twelve of sixteen starts. Northern Dancer was her grandsire.

RISEN STAR, the best son of Secretariat, was voted champion three-year-old of 1988. In the Kentucky Derby he encounted traffic problems and had to settle for third place behind Winning Colors and Forty Niner. Astute observers knew that the Derby was not a true bill because he had just defeated Forty Niner in the Lexington Stakes. After a comfortable victory in the Preakness., Risen Star turned in a tour de force in the Belmont, winning by nearly fifteen lengths! His clocking made it the second-fastest Belmont ever run. Only his phenomenal sire had been faster. Risen Star never raced again. He won eight of eleven starts.

WINNING COLORS in 1988 became just the third filly ever to capture the Kentucky Derby. She previously had won the Santa Anita Derby and the Santa Anita Oaks. On the strength of these three important victories, she was voted the best sophomore filly of the year. Winning Colors whipped a much stronger field in Kentucky than Genuine Risk had conquered. Forty Niner and Proper Reality (fourth) were good horses. Winning Colors was third in the Preakness.

PERSONAL ENSIGN was one of the ten greatest fillies of the century. She was never beaten in thirteen races, becoming the first undefeated horse with that many starts since Colin eighty years earlier. In a thrilling, unforgettable Breeders' Cup Distaff, she got up just in time to beat Winning Colors by a nose. Some people consider this Distaff the greatest race they ever saw, partly because of the exciting finish and partly because her perfect record was on the line. Personal Ensign had defeated Winning Colors more easily earlier in the Maskette. She outran males in the Whitney, but they were a bit less talented than the colts Winning Colors had beaten. Damascus and Hoist the Flag were the grandsires of Personal Ensign.

SUNDAY SILENCE and EASY GOER were intense rivals in 1989. They were more than just good horses; they were exceptional. They met four times, with Sunday Silence winning three. His first victory was a fairly comfortable one in the Kentucky Derby. The Preakness, however, was much closer, and Sunday Silence won only by a nose. Easy Goer turned the tables in the Belmont, frolicking home by eight lengths. It could be that Easy Goer had a home court advantage because he was based in New York. Or it could be that Sunday Silence couldn't handle the distance. We don't consider it necessary to be able to go a mile and a half. Spectacular Bid couldn't win at that distance, and we doubt that Dr. Fager could have.

The Breeders' Cup Classic was the climactic showdown event that would decide the Horse of the Year title. Easy Goer came flying down the stretch, but Sunday Silence held him off and won by a neck in track-record time. In the Gotham Stakes back in April, Easy Goer ran the fastest mile ever by a three-year-old, winning by thirteen lengths. He was first or second in nineteen of twenty starts. Sunday Silence was sent to Japan for stud duty, where he became the greatest sire that country has ever had.

1980 – 1985

96.6	Sunny's Halo
96.4	Interco
	Play Fellow
96.2	Desert Wine
96.0	Perrault
	John Henry
	Caveat
95.8	All Along (f.)
	Swale
	It's the One
	Slew o' Gold
95.6	April Run (f.)
	Althea (f.)
	Precisionist
	Conquistador Cielo
	Aloma's Ruler
	Bates Motel
95.4	Royal Heroine (f.)
	Majesty's Prince
	Track Barron
	Wild Again
	At the Threshold
	Lord at War
	Fali Time

	Prince True
	Spanish Drums
	Island Whirl
95.2	Star Choice
	Win
	Thunder Puddles
	Lemhi Gold
	Vanlandingham
	Gate Dancer
	Estrapade (f.)
	Linkage
	Summing
	Codex
	Bold 'n Determined (f.)
	Plugged Nickle
95.0	Cozzene
	Erins Isle
	Greinton
	Skip Trial
	Creme Fraiche
	Gato Del Sol
	Willow Hour
	Temperence Hill
	Genuine Risk (f.)
	Colonel Moran
94.8	Princess Rooney (f.)
	Heatherten (f.)
	Carr de Naskra
	Pleasant Colony
	Highland Blade
94.6	Life's Magic (f.)

1985 – 1990

98.2	Sunday Silence
98.0	Easy Goer
96.6	Spend a Buck
	Risen Star
96.4	Alysheba
	Snow Chief
96.2	Tank's Prospect
	Personal Ensign (f.)
	Bet Twice
	Ferdinand
	Java Gold
	Miesque (f.)
96.0	Chief's Crown
	Skywalker
	Winning Colors (f.)
	Lost Code
	Cutlass Reality
95.8	Eternal Prince
	Turkoman
	Forty Niner
	Cryptoclearance
	Manila
95.6	Proud Truth
	Precisionist

Blushing John
Seeking the Gold
Brian's Time
Private Terms
Storm Cat
Polish Navy
Sharrood
95.4   Wild Again
Garthorn
Proper Reality
Danzig Connection
Gulch
Theatrical
95.2   Lady's Secret (f.)
Broad Brush
Estrapade (f.)
95.0   Creme Fraiche
Skip Trial
Ogygian
94.8   Mogambo
94.6   Groovy

1990 – 1999

BAYAKOA was an Argentine mare who came to America and won titles at ages five and six. This battle-scared veteran was the same age as Personal Ensign and Miesque, but she did not develop as early as they. Her thirteen Grade I victories were a twentieth-century record for females. She went through a period of nineteen races in which she won fifteen and was unfairly weighted in the four that she lost.

GO FOR WAND was a young filly who was a champion both at two and at three. Her record of ten wins in thirteen starts is excellent. The 1990 Breeders' Cup Distaff was supposed to decide who was the best female in the country. The race was very competitive for the first mile, but then tragedy struck. Go for Wand broke her leg and had to be euthanized. Bayakoa went on to win the race, becoming the first female to win the Distaff twice.

CRIMINAL TYPE was named 1990 Horse of the Year, but we don't like the fact that his most important victories were achieved with weight advantages. When he upset Sunday Silence in the Hollywood Gold Cup, he was getting five pounds and won by a head. When he defeated future champion Housebuster in the Metropolitan, his advantage was seven pounds on the scale, and he won by a neck. Criminal Type lost twice to Ruhlmann when the weights were fair, and he beat that rival twice when the weights were not fair.

BLACK TIE AFFAIR captured the 1991 Horse of the Year title the old-fashioned way: he earned it. During his championship season he defeated such good horses as Housebuster, Farma Way, Summer Squall, Twilight Agenda and Unbridled. He won at five different tracks in 1991 and nine different tracks in his career. A late developer, he did not get really good until he was five. He won his last six races in a row, culminating with a victory in the Breeders' Cup Classic.

BEST PAL ran for six years and earned more than five million dollars. He was one of the best horses who never won a title. He did not do well in the 1991 Triple Crown events, but later races made it clear that he had not been at his best that spring. He did not really blossom until after a trainer switch to Gary Jones.

In the 1991 Pacific Classic, Best Pal proved that he could beat the same horses that Black Tie Affair whipped in the Breeders' Cup Classic. His most successful year was 1992, wherein he won four times and was unfairly weighted in the only race he lost. In the 1993 Hollywood Gold Cup he defeated Bertrando, who became a champion. His last great race was the 1995 Santa Anita Handicap, which he lost by a head under unfair weights.

A.P. INDY became Horse of the Year at three in 1992, mostly because he won the prestigious Breeders' Cup Classic, tying the stakes record. His second most important victory was the Belmont, in which he defeated the European horse My Memoirs and Preakness winner Pine Bluff. All these horses were flattered in 1993 when Lil E. Tee, who had lost the Arkansas Derby to Pine Bluff, outran Best Pal in the Oaklawn Handicap. A.P. Indy won eight of eleven races, including seven in a row. He may have been the best-bred horse of the century! His sire was Seattle Slew, and his broodmare sire was Secretariat. As expected, he became an outstanding sire himself.

LURE and KOTASHAAN were two important grass horses of the nineties. Lure won the Breeders' Cup Mile twice, and Kotashaan took the Breeders' Cup Turf, which brought him the 1993 Horse of the Year award. Lure never won a title, but some people thought he should have. He beat Paradise Creek in five of their seven encounters, and that horse became grass champion in 1994. Lure's grandsires were Northern Dancer and Alydar. In Europe, Kotashaan was third in the 1991 Grand Prix de Paris, a Group I race.

ARCANGUES became famous for winning the 1993 Breeders' Cup Classic at the astronomical odds of 133.60 to 1! He really shouldn't have been such a huge longshot. Bettors were careless and let a pot of gold get away. They should have noticed that in 1991 Arcangues had outrun Kotashaan, who had just won the 1993 Breeders' Cup Turf as the favorite. This is known as "back class." The talented Bertrando finished second in the Classic, followed by Kissin Kris and Marquetry. It was a fine field that Arcangues beat, confirming that he really was a good horse.

HOLY BULL was one of the best horses of the nineties in terms of his record. He won thirteen of sixteen starts, opening his career with five straight victories and later on winning six in a row. He was the favorite for the 1994 Kentucky Derby but finished twelfth. Holy Bull beat older horses twice in 1994, in the Metropolitan and in the Woodward. He did fine in some respects, but in others his career seems a little unsatisfying. He skipped the Breeders' Cup Classic, skipped the Belmont, skipped the Preakness, and was a flop in the Derby. Compare that to A.P. Indy, who won the Classic and won the only Triple Crown race he entered.

CIGAR is the only nineties star who was a Horse of the Year twice, in 1995 and 1996. He was a perfect ten-for-ten in 1995, becoming just the third horse to go undefeated in the handicap division, following in the footsteps of Tom Fool and Spectacular Bid. However, he never carried more than 126 pounds that year, even though he was five.

In 1996 Cigar captured the inaugural running of the ultra-rich Dubai World Cup, his presence in the new race lending it much prestige. In the Citation Challenge four months later, Cigar won his sixteenth consecutive victory, equaling a record set by Citation in 1950. Cigar was clearly the best horse of the nineties, but we don't consider him as good as Bold Ruler, the fifth best horse of the fifties. Cigar won nineteen of thirty-three races. In the same number of starts, Bold Ruler won twenty-three, despite carrying higher weights and facing more difficult competition. Cigar earned not quite ten million dollars, which was a new American record.

SERENA'S SONG was the champion three-year-old filly of 1995 and the highest money-winning female of her era. She had the same record as Skip Away – eighteen wins in thirty-eight starts – and she had one more Grade I win than he. Serena's Song was remarkably successful against males. In the Jim Beam she defeated Tejano Run, who ran second to champion Thunder Gulch in the Kentucky Derby. In the

Haskell she vanquished Pyramid Peak, who was second to Thunder Gulch in the Travers. Here then was a female champion who could beat the same horses as the male champion! At four she lost the Whitney by a neck while spotting the winning male eight pounds on the scale.

INSIDE INFORMATION won fourteen of seventeen starts – the same record as Seattle Slew. Her greatest victory was her last race, the Breeders' Cup Distaff, which she won by more than thirteen lengths over former champion Heavenly Prize. In the Beldame, Serena's Song had beaten that filly by less than one length. Serena's Song did not run her race in the Distaff, but Inside Information won so overwhelmingly that it seems unlikely that Serena could have caught her even if she had run better. Inside Information won nine races by more than five lengths. Her grandsires were Damascus and Key to the Mint.

FAVORITE TRICK was the third juvenile male to be named Horse of the Year. He was the first one that was not a superhorse, the other two being Native Dancer and Secretariat. He won all eight of his starts in 1997 and snagged the award mostly because nobody else deserved it. Skip Away lost seven races, and Silver Charm did not win after May. Favorite Trick managed to win two Grade 2 races in 1998, but he failed in both of his major goals. He ran eighth in the Kentucky Derby and eighth in the Breeders' Cup Mile.

SILVER CHARM was champion three-year-old of 1997 and a winner of nearly seven million dollars. The Kentucky Derby was his first important victory. In an exciting finish, he won by a head over Captain Bodgit, with Free House third. The Preakness was an even more thrilling finish, with all three stars heads apart at the wire. Silver Charm won again, with Free House second and Captain Bodgit third. This made him a heavy favorite to capture the Belmont, but he lost by less than a length to Touch Gold, with Free House third. In 1998 Silver Charm won the lucrative Dubai World Cup by a nose over foreign star Swain.

AWESOME AGAIN won the 1998 Breeders' Cup Classic over one of the best fields ever assembled. Silver Charm was second, Swain third, Victory Gallop fourth, Coronado's Quest fifth and Skip Away sixth. Silver Charm's margin over Swain was narrow, just as it had been in Dubai. This indicates that both those animals were trying their best and simply got outrun by a faster horse. Awesome Again won all his other races in 1998 as well. We consider him the best horse that ran that year. In his career he won nine of twelve races and more than $364,000 per start.

Bob Baffert, who trained Silver Charm, was back in the Triple Crown hunt in 1998 with REAL QUIET. This narrow-faced bay colt did not accomplish too much before the spring classics, nor afterward either, but Baffert had him at his best when it counted the most. Real Quiet captured both the Kentucky Derby and the Preakness, with Victory Gallop second both times. He was an odds-on favorite to take the Belmont and led in the race by as much as four lengths. Victory Gallop came with a tremendous kick in the stretch, however, and just managed to nip his rival at the wire by a whisker. It was for the best, as Real Quiet was never really accomplished enough to go down in history as a Triple Crown winner.

To us, VICTORY GALLOP was a hero, protecting the integrity of the Triple Crown. After Real Quiet left the stage for a while, Victory Gallop encountered a new rival, Coronado's Quest. This horse defeated him twice, first in the Haskell by about a length, and then in the Travers by only a nose. Victory Gallop retaliated by outrunning Coronado's Quest in the Breeders' Cup Classic. Real Quiet got the three-year-old title, but Victory Gallop went on to become champion handicap horse of 1999.

SKIP AWAY was a champion three times and a Horse of the Year in 1998, but he won these titles because he was exceptionally sound. He could always outearn his rivals, but he could not consistently beat them when he met them on the track. Louis Quatorze, Gentlemen and Formal Gold were all troublesome adversaries. Skip Away defeated these rivals six times, but he also lost to them six times at fair weights. He couldn't dominate. He was just one of a quartet of horses who were all about equal in ability.

Many people, confusing durability with ability, thought that Skip Away threw in a bad race in the 1998 Breeders' Cup Classic. We disagree. We think he finished sixth because he was the sixth best horse in the race. The five animals who outran him all were horses he had never faced. We can prove that he was not as good as Silver Charm. And if he was not as good as Silver Charm, there is no reason to think that he was as good as Swain or Victory Gallop or Coronado's Quest either.

We have already pointed out that Skip Away was similar in ability to Gentlemen. We also pointed out that Free House usually lost to Silver Charm. If Skip Away was better than Silver Charm, that would make Gentlemen better than Free House. However, when those two horses met in the 1998 Pacific Classic, it was Free House who triumphed over Gentlemen! Skip Away's greatest success was a surprise victory over Cigar in the 1996 Jockey Club Gold Cup. However, Cigar was no longer at his best after July of 1996. Otherwise he would not have lost three of his last four starts.

CHARISMATIC in 1999 pulled off quite a coup by being named Horse of the Year despite a slim resume. He was an important winner for only one month! He took the Lexington Stakes in mid-April, and he won the Preakness in mid-May. In between, he captured the Kentucky Derby. Before the Lexington, he had never won a stake, and he had appeared in one claiming race. Voters decided that his one month of excellence was enough to entitle him to the award. He was injured in the Belmont and retired. As with Tim Tam, we are confident he would have lost the Belmont anyway. He just didn't have the credentials of a Triple Crown winner. In fact, Tim Tam's credentials were better. He won ten of fourteen races. Charismatic won five of seventeen.

The twentieth century was horse racing's golden period. From Colin to Man o' War to Citation to Kelso to Secretariat, the great ones galloped across the pages of history and into our minds and hearts. The walls of the National Museum of Racing reverberate with the memories of their phenomenal achievements. Because of the infrequent starts and early retirements of modern horses, we are unlikely to witness anything like the twentieth century ever again.

1990 – 1995

96.8	A.P. Indy
96.6	Holy Bull
96.4	Pine Bluff
96.2	Lil E. Tee
96.0	Arcangues
	Best Pal
	Sea Hero
	Black Tie Affair
	In Excess
95.8	Bertrando
	Prairie Bayou
	Olympio
	Twilight Agenda
	Farma Way
95.6	Lure
	Star Recruit
	Kissin Kris
	Cherokee Run
	Hansel
	Dinard
	Unbridled
	Summer Squall
	Housebuster
	Ruhlmann

95.4   Kotashaan
Paradise Creek
The Wicked North
Miner's Mark
Corporate Report
Sea Cadet
Marquetry
Jolie's Halo
Criminal Type

95.2   Bien Bien
Soul of the Matter
Devil His Due
Colonial Affair
Fly So Free
Strike the Gold
Festin
Pleasant Tap
Miss Alleged (f.)

95.0   Brocco
Concern
Flag Down

94.8   Bayakoa (f.)
Go for Wand (f.)
Tabasco Cat

94.6   Hatoof (f.)
Unaccounted For
Dramatic Gold

94.4   Hollywood Wildcat (f.)
Flawlessly (f.)

94.2   Paseana (f.)

1995 – 1999

98.6	Cigar
96.8	Awesome Again
	Touch Gold
96.6	Silver Charm
96.4	Real Quiet
	Swain
	Captain Bodgit
	Free House
96.2	Victory Gallop
	Coronado's Quest
96.0	Gentlemen
	Formal Gold
	Alphabet Soup
	Skip Away
	Louis Quatorze
95.8	Siphon
95.6	Geri
95.4	Lemon Drop Kid
	Helmsman
95.2	Charismatic
	Vision and Verse
	Soul of the Matter
	Tinners Way
95.0	Inside Information (f.)

	Menifee
94.8	Thunder Gulch
	Serena's Song (f.)
	Cat Thief
94.6	Dramatic Gold
	Wekiva Springs
	Unaccounted For
	Pyramid Peak
94.4	Heavenly Prize (f.)
	Star Standard
94.2	Favorite Trick
	Paseana (f.)
	Sky Beauty (f.)

Unusual Historical Facts

1. At least two thirties horses have movies about their exploits, Phar Lap (foreign) and Seabiscuit.

2. In the fall of 1936, Roman Soldier won four different stakes at four different Maryland tracks–Laurel, Havre de Grace, Pimlico, Bowie – all within less than a month.

3. Seven Hearts, a totally forgotten horse of the mid-forties, won twenty-seven races and had a higher winning percentage than Whirlaway.

4. Although he had just won the Kentucky Derby and Preakness, Assault was not the favorite in the 1946 Belmont. That honor went to Lord Boswell, who was a flop in the big race.

5. In the 1946-47 Experimental Handicap, a filly, First Flight, headed the list of colts.

6. On January 5, 1949, the thoroughbred Olympia outsprinted a noted quarter horse in a quarter-mile match race.

7. Within just thirteen years, Pensive, his son Ponder, and his grandson Needles all won the Kentucky Derby.

8. Battlefield finished first or second in twenty-six of his first twenty-seven starts, 1950-52.

9. Alerted made sixty-four starts in just two years (1951-52). That's more starts than Kelso made in his entire career!

10. Imbros, son of the speedster Polynesian and sire of the speedster Native Diver, posted two world records in 1954.

11. The tireless campaigner Social Outcast competed in eighteen stakes in 1955 alone.

12. Summer Tan, the century's unluckiest horse, finished second in eleven stakes.

13. Silky Sullivan, the century's most extreme stretch runner, could come from forty-one lengths behind to win! He was a very popular horse in 1958.

14. Vertex (1956-59) ran for four years and never had a losing season. Altogether he won seventeen of twenty-five races.

15. In 1959, Silver Spoon won the Santa Anita Derby and then ran in the Kentucky Derby, wherein she finished fifth of seventeen. She took on the boys again in the Cinema Handicap and won.

16. 1960 Preakness winner Bally Ache was in the money in twenty-nine straight races.

17. In the seventies, the Kentucky Derby was won twice by horses who had competed abroad: Canonero II (Venezuela) and Bold Forbes (Puerto Rico).

18. Match races are supposed to bring together evenly matched horses. Not so in 1974, when Chris Evert defeated Miss Musket by fifty lengths!

19. Ancient Title ran seven furlongs seven times (1972-75) and was never beaten at this distance.

20. Susan's Girl, who won three titles (1972-75), was beaten seven times by Tizna, who did not win any titles.

21. Davona Dale in 1979 became the only filly ever to win both the old Triple Tiara and the new one, a feat requiring her to sweep five important races in a row.

22. Forty Niner (1987-88) was one of history's most tenacious competitors. He won four stakes by a nose and was in nine races decided by a neck or less.

23. Flawlessly, the best daughter of Affirmed, captured the important Matriarch Stakes three years in a row, 1991-93.

24. Bertrando (1991-94) was so quick that he led at the first call in twenty-one straight races!

25. Hansel and Charismatic were alike in that they captured two-thirds of the Triple Crown but never won any other Grade 1 stakes.

KEEPING THINGS IN PERSPECTIVE

If you love racing history, here are a few things to keep in mind:

1. The Horse of the Year is not always the best horse. He is the one who is thought to have had the best year. LADY'S SECRET was not the best horse that ran in 1986, nor was FAVORITE TRICK the best in 1997 – but the voters felt that they had had the best year. CHALLEDON won two Horse of the Year titles, even though he was never the best horse, except during periods when JOHNSTOWN and EIGHT THIRTY were out of action.

2. It's easier for fillies to beat colts when they are two because sometimes the males are slower to develop. TOP FLIGHT and BEWITCH could beat good colts as juveniles, but they had no such luck in later years. The greatest fillies are those who can beat outstanding males beyond age two. TWILIGHT TEAR, BUSHER, REGRET and BUG BRUSH did this. WAYA and IMP could at least hold their own against the best males of their day. Of course, the weights must be fair. Otherwise, the winner is not the best horse. This criterion eliminates such overrated females as GALLORETTE and ESPOSA. Winning a Grade 1 stake that is restricted to fillies is not nearly as impressive as winning a Grade 1 race, at fair weights, in open company.

3. One should not regard graded stakes as equivalent in different years. They're not. In certain years, the Jockey Club Gold Cup attracted wonderful fields. But in other years, the best horses did not want to go two miles, so they boycotted the race. SHUVEE gained a lot of prestige from winning this event twice, but the

fields she beat were substandard. Even the Kentucky Derby can have a weak field, as it did in 1951, 1974 and 1980.

4. Winning a ton of money does not make a horse great. STYMIE is a good example of this. In six years on the track, he never had a season in which he won as many races as he lost. Some fans get confused because he had several wins over ASSAULT – but those were in marathons. ASSAULT, although he won the Belmont (in slow time vs. a moderate field), was not really a distance horse. All his other attempts to go beyond ten furlongs were failures. Yet the Brooklyn and Butler Handicaps proved that he was at least nine pounds better than STYMIE. DEVIL DIVER was thirteen pounds better than STYMIE.

5. "Beating older horses" is an overrated achievement. It implies that the oldsters are superior to the youngsters, but often they are not. Consider the 1979 Marlboro Cup. Three-year-olds grabbed all the top prizes: SPECTACULAR BID, GENERAL ASSEMBLY and COASTAL. In 1983, SLEW O' GOLD won a title mostly because he beat his elders in the fall, yet he did not dominate his own crop. He lost the Kentucky Derby to SUNNY'S HALO, the Belmont to CAVEAT, and the Travers to PLAY FELLOW. The three-year-olds were just better than the older horses that year. One reason that the sophomores are sometimes superior to their elders is that the best horses of the previous crop often retire.

   As horses get older, they tend to improve as they get bigger and stronger. That might make one think that they would have an edge over the youngsters. However, the Scale of Weights is designed to nullify their advantage. Our research has shown that most males peak when they are six. This was true of WHISK BROOM II, IRON MASK, OLD ROSEBUD, SUN BEAU, ARMED, FORT MARCY, FOREGO, ROYAL GLINT, JOHN HENRY, probably STYMIE, and conceivably NATIVE DIVER. SEABISCUIT and CIGAR peaked when they were five; EXTERMINATOR peaked when he was seven. It's hard to say when KELSO peaked, but he had a very good year when he was six.

6. The winning percentage you should expect of a great horse depends on his number of starts. The more a horse runs, the more his percentage drops. No undefeated horse in America had more than fifteen starts (COLIN). The best horses with about twenty starts – MAN O' WAR and NATIVE DANCER – each had one defeat. Because of his many speed records, his money record, and the weight he toted, MAN O' WAR was the most accomplished horse with a short career. The best horses with a middle-sized career (about thirty starts) win at least seventy percent of their races. The most accomplished of these was AFFIRMED. He was a Triple Crown winner, a world-record earner, a champion every year he ran, and a Horse of the Year twice.

   Among horses with long careers (about sixty starts), the greatest was five-time champion KELSO. He and the great FOREGO won about sixty percent of their races. That's the best a horse can do when he's regularly conceding huge amounts of weight. Horses with very long careers (eighty or so starts) are lucky to win even half their races. ARMED and OLD ROSEBUD were able to accomplish this feat. EXTERMINATOR, who raced 100 times, also managed to win half. However, these three were not in the same league as KELSO or FOREGO.

THE TOP TWENTY

1. Man o' War
2. Native Dancer
3. Citation
4. Kelso
5. Secretariat
6. Seattle Slew
7. Affirmed
8. Spectacular Bid
9. Dr. Fager
10. Forego
11. Colin
12. Count Fleet
13. Sysonby
14. Damascus
15. Buckpasser
16. Swaps
17. Nashua
18. Tom Fool
19. Seabiscuit
20. War Admiral

EXPLANATION OF THE RANKINGS

There never was another horse like MAN O' WAR. Consistency? Speed? Weight? Margins? Earnings? He could do it all. But experts tend to underestimate NATIVE DANCER. They forget what he was. He came within a head of being the ultimate superhorse of all time: a never-beaten Triple Crown winner! CITATION'S somewhat disappointing record as an older horse places him below NATIVE DANCER. However, that record becomes irrelevant when you compare him to SECRETARIAT because that superstar did not run beyond age three. Surely CITATION'S 27-2 record in his first two years is a lot more impressive than SECRETARIAT's 16-5.

KELSO also won sixteen of twenty-one races between the summer of 1960 and the summer of 1962. However, a lot of his starts were in handicaps in which he had to concede considerable weight. Then factor in everything that KELSO accomplished afterward, and you can see that his total achievement outranks that of SECRETARIAT. Our top five horses all had world records.

SEATTLE SLEW and AFFIRMED did not, but they are the only two besides SECRETARIAT who were great enough to sweep the Triple Crown over a period of sixty-six years. Although AFFIRMED accomplished more than SEATTLE SLEW, the latter takes precedence because of the result of their confrontation in the Marlboro Cup. Similarly, AFFIRMED outranks SPECTACULAR BID because of the result of their clash in the Jockey Club Gold Cup. Since most of the great ones never met, we take it very seriously when they did meet.

Unlike the top seven horses, SPECTACULAR BID and DR. FAGER never won beyond a mile and a quarter, nor did they capture the Triple Crown. However, like all of the top seven except CITATION and KELSO, who had long careers, SPECTACULAR BID was a champion every year he ran, whereas DR. FAGER was a champ only in one year. Both horses lost four times, but SPECTACULAR BID won twenty-six races as against eighteen for DR. FAGER. The good DOCTOR was a sensational four-year-old, much more impressive than FOREGO was at the same age. DR. FAGER was also more successful at three. FOREGO took a long time to blossom fully. Even so, when you look at the sum-total of everything he accomplished over many years, he surely deserves to outrank COLIN, who made only three starts beyond the age of two.

Like COLIN, COUNT FLEET did not run much beyond age two—just six times. He lost five races in his complete career, whereas COLIN did not lose at all. COUNT FLEET and SYSONBY both ended their careers with ten straight victories. Although SYSONBY had the better record (only one defeat), we are giving the edge to COUNT FLEET on the basis of his Triple Crown, his fast times, and the fact that many of SYSONBY's toughest opponents were females. SYSONBY's splendid record was much better than that of DAMASCUS, who lost eleven times. The latter's record was not as good as BUCKPASSER's, but he takes precedence because of his ten-length victory over that formidable rival in the Woodward Stakes.

BUCKPASSER's 25-6 record is substantially better than those of the next three horses in the rankings, and he won more titles than they did. SWAPS was placed ahead of NASHUA because both horses seemed to be in fine fettle in the Kentucky Derby, whereas some claimed that SWAPS was not at his best physically during their match race. It would seem that SWAPS at four was better than NASHUA at three. NASHUA was a much better three-year-old than TOM FOOL, but the latter was better at four. We have listed NASHUA first because he earned more than twice as much money as TOM FOOL, even though there was only a few years' difference in their ages. Even as four-year-olds, NASHUA won more money.

TOM FOOL was a greater four-year-old than SEABISCUIT. NASHUA was able to become a world's leading money winner within thirty starts; SEABISCUIT required almost ninety starts to achieve the same thing. He, of course, outranks WAR ADMIRAL because of his victory over that archrival in their famous match race. TOM FOOL also can be seen to be better than WAR ADMIRAL. Both horses had an undefeated season, but TOM FOOL's occurred in the handicap division, where he had to concede much weight. Both horses won a triple crown of sorts, but TOM FOOL's crown has been more rarely won. TOM FOOL won two titles; WAR ADMIRAL, only one.

WEIGHT – CARRYING PROWESS

SPRINTS			ROUTES
150	Iron Mask (6)	139	Discovery (4)
147	Roseben (4)	139	Whisk Broom II (6)
146	Pan Zareta (5 f.)	138	Man o' War (3)
142	Ta Wee (4 f.)	138	Exterminator (7)
142	King James (4)	137	Forego (6)
140	Devil Diver (3)	136	Bold Ruler (3)
140	Roman (4)	136	several 4-yr.-olds

WORLD   RECORD   HOLDERS

WORLD	RECORD	HOLDERS
Artful (F.)	Gen. Duke	Noor
Buckpasser	Honeymoon (F.)	Pan Zareta (F.)
Bug Brush (F.)	Imbros	Polynesian
Challedon	Intentionally	Riva Ridge
Citation	Iron Mask	Roseben
Clang	John Henry	Round Table
Coaltown	Lucky Draw	Secretariat
Crystal Water	Man o' War	Sir Barton
Discovery	Native Dancer	Swaps
Dr. Fager	Native Diver	Waya (F.)
Equipoise		Whisk Broom II

LEADING　　MONEY　　WINNERS

LEADING	MONEY	WINNERS
Man o' War	Assault	Kelso
Zev	Armed	Affirmed
Gallant Fox	Stymie	Spectacular Bid
Sun Beau	Citation	John Henry
Seabiscuit	Nashua	Alysheba
Whirlaway	Round Table	Cigar

TRIPLE	CROWN	WINNERS
Sir Barton	Whirlaway	Secretariat
Gallant Fox	Count Fleet	Seattle Slew
Omaha	Assault	Affirmed
War Admiral	Citation	

HANDICAP	TRIPLE	CROWN
Whisk Broom II	Tom Fool	Kelso

BIGGEST WINNING MARGINS

Man o' War	100 lengths
Chris Evert (F.)	50
Secretariat	31
Count Fleet	30
Discovery	
Imp (F.)	
Damascus	22
Roseben	20
Go For Wand (F.)	18 1/4
Princess Rooney (F.)	18
Bold Forbes	17
Spectacular Bid	
Althea (F.)	15
Arts and Letters	
Autobiography	
Hoist the Flag	
Ruffian (F.)	
Spend a Buck	
Risen Star	14 3/4
Conquistador Cielo	14
Honest Pleasure	
John Henry	
Never Bend	
Bertrando	13 1/2

Inside Information (F.)
Alydar   13
Easy Goer
Gun Bow
Housebuster

LONGEST WINNING STREAKS

Cigar	16 races
Citation	
Buckpasser	15
Colin	
Man o' War	14
Personal Ensign (F)	13
Gallant Bloom (F)	12
Spectacular Bid	
Kelso	11
Native Dancer	
Old Rosebud	
Round Table	
Tom Fool	
Twilight Tear (F)	
War Admiral	
Alsab	10
Count Fleet	
Mac Diarmida	
Princess Rooney (F)	
Ruffian (F)	
Sarazen	
Sysonby	
Affirmed	9
Favorite Trick	

Foolish Pleasure
Hermis
Honest Pleasure
Majestic Prince
Manila
Seattle Slew   9
Skip Away
Swaps
Zev

High Winning Percentages

100.0	Colin
100.0	Personal Ensign (F.)
95.5	Native Dancer
95.2	Man o' War
93.3	Sysonby
90.9	Ruffian (F.)
90.0	Majestic Prince
86.7	Spectacular Bid
83.3	Hoist the Flag
82.4	Seattle Slew
82.4	Inside Information (F.)
81.8	Dr. Fager
81.8	Regret (F.)
81.3	Holy Bull
81.0	Princess Rooney (F.)
80.8	War Admiral
80.6	Buckpasser
80.0	Real Delight (F.)
77.8	Northern Dancer
77.8	Burgomaster
77.8	Commando
76.9	Go For Wand (F.)
76.2	Secretariat
76.2	Count Fleet

76.0	Swaps
75.9	Affirmed
75.0	Twilight Tear (F.)
75.0	Miesque (F.)
75.0	Mac Diarmida
75.0	Top Flight (F.)
75.0	Morvich
75.0	Awesome Again
75.0	Artful (F.)
73.3	Nashua
73.3	Bimelech
72.7	Gallant Bloom (F.)
72.7	A. P. Indy
72.7	Risen Star
72.2	Bold Forbes
71.4	Busher (F.)
71.4	Ta Wee (F.)
71.4	Sky Beauty (F.)
71.4	Tim Tam
71.1	Citation
70.6	Maskette (F.)
70.5	Fitz Herbert
70.4	Ack Ack
70.0	Tom Fool
70.0	Easy Goer
69.7	Bold Ruler

Measuring Equine Success

The most successful horses are not always the most talented, but what they achieve is certainly worthy of praise. You can measure their success via a simple mathematical formula. Just multiply their earnings by their winning percentage. These two factors neatly counterbalance each other. It's easier for a horse to make a lot of money if he has a lot of starts, but it's easier for him to maintain a high winning percentage if he does not have very many starts.

Here are the ten most successful horses of each decade:

1900 - 09	1910 - 19
1. Colin	1. Billy Kelly
2. Sysonby	2. Sir Barton
3. Ballot	3. Sweep
4. Peter Pan	4. Boniface
5. Artful (F.)	5. Roamer
6. Beldame (F.)	6. Old Rosebud
7. Maskette (F.)	7. The Porter
8. Burgomaster	8. Jack Atkin
9. Hamburg Belle (F.)	9. Cudgel
10. Commando	10. Regret (F.)

1920 - 29	1930 - 39
1. Man o' War	1. War Admiral

2. Blue Larkspur
3. Zev
4. Exterminator
5. Morvich
6. Victorian
7. Sarazen
8. Osmand
9. Crusader
10. Reigh Count

2. Gallant Fox
3. Top Flight (F.)
4. Equipoise
5. Sun Beau
6. Seabiscuit
7. Challedon
8. Twenty Grand
9. Whichone
10. Jamestown

1940 - 49

1. Citation
2. Armed
3. Whirlaway
4. Assault
5. Coaltown
6. Stymie
7. Busher (F.)
8. Count Fleet
9. Ponder
10. Bimelech

1950 - 59

1. Round Table
2. Nashua
3. Native Dancer
4. Swaps
5. Swoon's Son
6. Bold Ruler
7. First Landing
8. Tom Fool
9. Bardstown
10. Hillsdale

1960 - 69

1. Kelso
2. Buckpasser
3. Dr. Fager
4. Damascus
5. Native Diver
6. Northern Dancer
7. Candy Spots

1970 - 79

1. Spectacular Bid
2. Affirmed
3. Forego
4. Secretariat
5. Seattle Slew
6. Exceller
7. Foolish Pleasure

8. Cicada (F.)
9. Carry Back
10. In Reality

8. Riva Ridge
9. Susan's Girl (F.)
10. Flying Paster

1980 - 89

1. Easy Goer
2. Sunday Silence
3. John Henry
4. Alysheba
5. Spend a Buck
6. Slew o' Gold
7. Snow Chief
8. Manila
9. Personal Ensign (F.)
10. Lady's Secret (F.)

1990 - 99

1. Cigar
2. Skip Away
3. Silver Charm
4. Awesome Again
5. Best Pal
6. A. P. Indy
7. Holy Bull
8. Gentlemen
9. Paradise Creek
10. Victory Gallop

THE BEST HORSES WHO SIRED OR GRANDSIRED OTHER TOP HORSES:

Affirmed	Fair Play	Polynesian
Alydar	Friar Rock	Ponder
Attention	Gallant Fox	Pretense
Bald Eagle	Gallant Man	Quadrangle
Ballot	Hasty Road	Reigh Count
Battlefield	Hill Prince	Rosemont
Blue Larkspur	Hoist the Flag	Round Table
Bold Ruler	Imbros	Seattle Slew
Bold Venture	Intentionally	Secretariat
Buckpasser	Jack High	Shut Out
Bull Lea	Jamestown	Skywalker
Chance Play	John P. Grier	Swaps
Citation	Johnstown	Swoon's Son
Commando	Key to the Mint	Sword Dancer
Count Fleet	Majestic Prince	The Finn
Crafty Admiral		
Damascus	Man o' War	Tim Tam
Devil Diver	Nashua	Tom Fool
Discovery	Native Dancer	T. V. Lark

Eight Thirty	Never Bend	Vertex
Equipoise	Northern Dancer	War Admiral
	Pensive	Whisk Broom II
		Your Host

NOTED GELDINGS

Ancient Title	Fort Marcy	Roamer
Armed	John Henry	Roman Brother
Azucar	Kelso	Roseben
Bardstown	Lucky Draw	Royal Glint
Best Pal	Marriage	Sarazen
Clang	Native Diver	Social Outcast
Exterminator	Old Rosebud	Tiller
Forego	Quicken Tree	

The Twenty Best Females

All Along	Imp
Artful	Maskette
Beldame	Miesque
Black Helen	Nimba
Brookdale Nymph	Personal Ensign
Bug Brush	Regret
Busher	Ruffian
Dahlia	Twilight Tear
Desert Vixen	Waya
Gallant Bloom	Winning Colors

THE TWENTY BEST GRASS HORSES

All Along (f.)	Majestic Light
Bowl Game	Manila
Caucasus	Miesque (f.)
Cougar II	Mongo
Dahlia (f.)	Perrault
Exceller	Round Table
John Henry	The Axe II
Johnny D.	Tiller
King Pellinore	T. V. Lark
Mac Diarmida	Waya (f.)

THE BEST WHO WON 2/3 OF THE TRIPLE CROWN

Alysheba	Northern Dancer
Bold Venture	Pensive
Capot	Real Quiet
Damascus	Risen Star
Johnstown	Riva Ridge
Majestic Prince	Shut Out
Man o' War	Silver Charm
Middleground	Spectacular Bid
Nashua	Sunday Silence
Native Dancer	Twenty Grand

THE BEST WHO WON THE KENTUCKY DERBY ONLY

Agile
Black Gold
Cavalcade
Determine
Exterminator
Ferdinand
Foolish Pleasure
George Smith
Iron Liege
Lil E. Tee

Lucky Debonair
Old Rosebud
Omar Khayyam
Regret (f.)
Reigh Count
Spend a Buck
Sunny's Halo
Swaps
Tomy Lee
Winning Colors (f.)

THE BEST WHO WON
THE PREAKNESS ONLY

Alsab

Bally Ache

Bold Ruler

Candy Spots

Challedon

Hasty Road

Head Play

High Quest

Hill Prince

Jack Hare Jr.

Louis Quatorze

Personality

Pine Bluff

Polynesian

Prairie Bayou

Snow Chief

Tank's Prospect

Tom Rolfe

Victorian

War Cloud

THE BEST WHO WON
THE BELMONT ONLY

A. P. Indy

Arts and Letters

Bet Twice

Colin

Commando

Counterpoint

Crusader

Easy Goer

Gallant Man

Granville

Grey Lag

Johren

Luke McLuke

One Count

Peter Pan

Stage Door Johnny

Sword Dancer

The Finn

Touch Gold

Victory Gallop

Outstanding In Sprints

Ack Ack	Jack High
Affectionately (f.)	Jamestown
Apache	Messenger of Song
Artful (f.)	Motor Cop
Berseem	Mr. Prospector
Billy Kelly	My Juliet (f.)
Bold Lad	Myrtlewood (f.)
Bold Ruler	Native Diver
Cherokee Run	Naturalist
Clang	Olympia
Coaltown	Osmand
Crocus (f.)	Pan Zareta (f.)
Devil Diver	Plugged Nickle
Dr. Fager	Polynesian
Federal Hill	Precisionist
First Flight (f.)	Raise a Native
Flying Heels	Roman
Forego	Roseben
Groovy	Sation
Gulch	Spy Song
Hamburg Belle (f.)	Star de Naskra
Housebuster	Ta Wee (f.)
Imbros	Tom Fool

Impressive

Intentionally

Iron Mask

Jack Atkin

White Skies

Wise Counsellor

With Pleasure

Worthmore

Outstanding In Marathons

Accountant	High Gun
Africander	Hill Prince
Alsab	Inside Tract
Arts and Letters	Kelso
Autobiography	Mad Hatter
Bit of White (f.)	Market Wise
Buckpasser	Nashua
Chance Play	Omaha
Citation	One Count
Count Arthur	Pavot
Counterpoint	Phalanx
Cravat	Ponder
Crusader	Pot o' Luck
Damascus	Princequillo
Dark Secret	Prove Out
Diavolo	Quicken Tree
Ethelbert	Reigh Count
Exceller	Roman Brother
Exterminator	Shorthose
Fenelon	Shuvee (f.)
Firethorn	Stymie
Forego	Sword Dancer
Gallant Fox	Sysonby

Gallant Man	Twenty Grand
Gusto	War Admiral
Hermis	Whirlaway

No horse born after 1973 made the list.

OUR NOMINEES FOR BEST HORSE OF SEASON

1900	Ethelbert, Imp (f.), Kinley Mack
1901	Commando, Imp (f.), Kilmarnock
1902	Gold Heels, Hermis
1903	Africander, Hermis, Waterboy
1904	Beldame (f.) Hermis, Irish Lad
1905	Artful (f.) Ort Wells, Sysonby
1906	Burgomaster, Go Between, Water Pearl
1907	Ballot, Colin, Peter Pan
1908	Ballot, Celt, Colin
1909	Fitz Herbert, King James, Maskette (f.)
1910	Fitz Herbert, King James, Sweep
1911	Meridian, Plate Glass, Zeus
1912	Free Lance, Plate Glass, The Manager
1913	Cock o' the Walk, Rock View, Whisk Broom II
1914	Borrow, Luke McLuke, Roamer
1915	Regret (f.), Roamer
1916	Friar Rock, George Smith, The Finn
1917	Hourless, Old Rosebud, Regret (f.)
1918	Cudgel, Johren, Sun Briar
1919	Cudgel, Sir Barton, Sun Briar

1920	Man o' War, Sir Barton
1921	Exterminator, Morvich
1922	Exterminator, Whiskaway
1923	Grey Lag, In Memorium, Zev
1924	Black Gold, Sarazen
1925	American Flag, Sting
1926	Crusader, Haste, Sarazen
1927	Chance Play, Mars, Nimba (f.)
1928	Nimba (f.), Osmand, Reigh Count
1929	Blue Larkspur, Osmand, Reigh Count
1930	Blue Larkspur, Gallant Fox, Jamestown
1931	Questionnaire, Top Flight (f.), Twenty Grand
1932	Burgoo King, Equipoise, Faireno
1933	Bazaar (f.), Dark Secret, Equipoise
1934	Cavalcade, Equipoise, High Quest
1935	Discovery, Omaha
1936	Bold Venture, Discovery, Granville
1937	Seabiscuit, War Admiral
1938	Seabiscuit, Stagehand, War Admiral
1939	Eight Thirty, Johnstown
1940	Bimelech, Eight Thirty, Seabiscuit
1941	Market Wise, Our Boots, Whirlaway
1942	Alsab, Shut Out, Whirlaway
1943	Count Fleet, Devil Diver, Market Wise
1944	Devil Diver, Pensive, Twilight Tear (f.)
1945	Armed, Busher (f.), Devil Diver
1946	Armed, Assault, First Flight (f.)
1947	Armed, Assault
1948	Blue Peter, Citation
1949	Capot, Coaltown

1950	Citation, Hill Prince, Noor
1951	Citation, Counterpoint
1952	Native Dancer, One Count, Spartan Valor
1953	Mark-Ye-Well, Native Dancer, Tom Fool
1954	Determine, Errard King, Native Dancer
1955	High Gun, Nashua, Swaps
1956	Nashua, Swaps, Swoon's Son
1957	Bold Ruler, Gallant Man, Traffic Judge
1958	Bold Ruler, Gallant Man, Round Table
1959	Bug Brush (f.), Hillsdale, Sword Dancer
1960	Bald Eagle, Kelso, T. V. Lark
1961	Kelso, Prove It, T. V. Lark
1962	Beau Purple, Kelso, Prove It
1963	Kelso, Mongo, Raise a Native
1964	Kelso, Mongo, Northern Dancer
1965	Kelso, Native Diver, Tom Rolfe
1966	Bold Lad, Buckpasser, Lucky Debonair
1967	Buckpasser, Damascus, Dr. Fager
1968	Damascus, Dr. Fager, Stage Door Johnny
1969	Arts and Letters, Majestic Prince, Top Knight
1970	Fort Marcy, Nodouble, Personality
1971	Ack Ack, Canonero II, Good Behaving
1972	Autobiography, Key to the Mint, Solar Salute
1973	Desert Vixen (f.), Prove Out, Secretariat
1974	Forego, Ruffian (f.)
1975	Forego, Wajima
1976	Bold Forbes, Dahlia (f.), Forego
1977	Crystal Water, Forego, Seattle Slew
1978	Affirmed, Exceller, Seattle Slew
1979	Affirmed, Spectacular Bid, Waya (f.)

1980	Spectacular Bid, Temperence Hill, Tiller
1981	Island Whirl, John Henry
1982	John Henry, Landaluce (f.), Perrault
1983	All Along (f.), Sunny's Halo
1984	Interco, Slew o' Gold, Swale
1985	Chief's Crown, Spend a Buck, Tank's Prospect
1986	Manila, Skywalker, Snow Chief
1987	Alysheba, Ferdinand, Snow Chief
1988	Alysheba, Personal Ensign (f.), Risen Star
1989	Easy Goer, Sunday Silence
1990	Housebuster, Ruhlmann, Unbridled
1991	Best Pal, Black Tie Affair, In Excess
1992	A.P. Indy, Best Pal, Lure
1993	Arcangues, Lil E. Tee, Sea Hero
1994	Holy Bull, Soul of the Matter, The Wicked North
1995	Cigar, Inside Information (f.), Thunder Gulch
1996	Alphabet Soup, Cigar, Skip Away
1997	Gentlemen, Silver Charm, Touch Gold
1998	Awesome Again, Real Quiet
1999	Charismatic, Lemon Drop Kid, Victory Gallop

THE GREATEST STAKES
AND WHO WON THEM

We picked the five greatest stakes for three-year-olds and the five greatest events for older horses, and then determined who won the races. How many of the best races did your favorite horse capture? Of course, it helps to have a long career over many seasons. As the years unfolded, some races declined in importance, while others gained in prestige. Therefore, we occasionally saw fit to replace certain stakes with new races. Most of the currently big events did not even exist in 1900.

For the three-year-olds, we started out with the Withers, Belmont, Lawrence Realization, Dwyer and Tidal Stakes. The first three of these were considered analogous to the English Triple Crown. The Kentucky Derby and Preakness were not so important then. We introduced the Derby in 1911 and the Preakness in 1918. By the thirties, the Withers and Lawrence Realization were losing status, so we replaced them with the Arlington Classic and Wood Memorial. In the fifties, we substituted the Florida Derby for the Wood. In the seventies, we replaced the Arlington Classic with the Travers.

For the older horses, we began with the Metropolitan, the Suburban, the Brooklyn, the First Special and the Second Special. When the latter pair were discontinued, we substituted the Saratoga Cup and the Saratoga Handicap, which we included until 1920, when the Jockey Club Gold Cup, still an important race today, was inaugurated. We used the Saratoga Cup until 1937, the first year of the Pimlico Special. That race was discontinued in the mid-fifties, around the time that the Woodward Stakes began.

All good things must come to an end, and by the mid-seventies the New York Handicap Triple was beginning to lose its importance. We therefore replaced the Metropolitan, Suburban and Brooklyn Handicaps with the Santa Anita Handicap, the Hollywood Gold Cup and the Marlboro Cup. We used the Marlboro until 1984, when it was replaced by the Breeders' Cup Classic. On the next pages, you will see the tabulation of how many prestigious races each horse won!

151

1900-09		1910-19		1920-29	
4	Fitz Herbert	6	Roamer	6	Exterminator
4	Ballot	4	Sir Barton	5	Man o' War
3	Colin	4	Johren	5	Mad Hatter
3	Sysonby	4	Omar Khayyam	4	Crusader
3	Fair Play	4	Friar Rock	4	Reigh Count
3	Peter Pan	3	Whisk Broom II	4	Grey Lag
3	Beldame (F.)	3	The Finn	4	Zev
3	Kinley Mack	3	Stromboli	3	Mad Play
3	Delhi	3	Rock View		
	Major				
3	Daingerfield	3	The Manager		
3	Accountant	3	Olambala		
3	Africander	3	Star Charter		

1930-39		1940-49		1950-59	
7	Gallant Fox	8	Assault	7	Nashua
5	War Admiral	6	Whirlaway	6	Sword Dancer
5	Twenty Grand	5	Citation	5	Native Dancer
4	Equipoise	5	Devil Diver	4	Tom Fool
4	Omaha	4	Count Fleet	4	High Gun
4	Challedon	4	Shut Out	3	Gallant Man
4	Dark Secret	4	Market Wise	3	Hill Prince
3	Discovery	3	Capot	3	Traffic Judge

3 Johnstown   3 Stymie   3 Tim Tam

3 Granville   3 Ponder   3 Needles

3 Firethorn   3 Phalanx

3 Cravat

1960-69		1970-79	
12	Kelso	11	Forego
6	Buckpasser	7	Affirmed
5	Damascus	5	Seattle Slew
4	Arts and Letters	4	Secretariat
4	Carry Back	3	Riva Ridge
3	Gun Bow	3	Key to the Mint
3	Northern Dancer		
3	Forward Pass		
3	Candy Spots		

1980-89		1990-99	
6	Spectacular Bid	5	Cigar
5	Alysheba	5	Skip Away
4	Easy Goer	4	Thunder Gulch
4	Slew o' Gold	3	Real Quiet
3	Sunday Silence	3	Holy Bull
3	Ferdinand	3	Unbridled
3	John Henry		
3	Swale		
3	Temperence Hill		
3	Creme Fraiche		
3	Pleasant Colony		

FEMALES WITH TWO RACES:
Twilight Tear, Nimba, Shuvee, Gallorette

Top Twenty Male Foal Crops

1. 1954 Bold Ruler, Gallant Man, Round Table, Gen. Duke, Vertex, Iron Liege

2. 1970 Secretariat, Forego, Sham, Our Native, Linda's Chief, Ancient Title

3. 1952 Swaps, Nashua, Saratoga, Bardstown, Traffic Judge, Summer Tan

4. 1975 Affirmed, Alydar, Mac Diarmida John Henry, Believe It, Nasty and Bold

5. 1964 Dr. Fager, Damascus, In Reality, Fort Marcy, Proud Clarion, Bold Hour

6. 1931 High Quest, Cavalcade, Discovery, King Saxon, Top Row, Time Supply

7. 1911 Old Rosebud, Luke McLuke, Roamer, Boots, Pennant, Stromboli

8. 1945 Citation, Noor, Coaltown, My Request, Vulcan's Forge, Better Self

9. 1957 Kelso, Prove It, Beau Purple,
T.V. Lark, Bally Ache, Venetian Way

10. 1905 Colin, Celt, Fair Play,
Hessian, King James, Sir John Johnson

11. 1939 Devil Diver, Shut Out, Alsab,
Sun Again, Requested, Valdina Orphan

12. 1938 Whirlaway, Our Boots, Market Wise,
Attention, War Relic, Riverland

13. 1974 Seattle Slew, Tiller, Johnny D.,
Bowl Game, Run Dusty Run, J. O. Tobin

14. 1994 Awesome Again, Touch Gold, Silver Charm, Captain
Bodgit, Free House, Pulpit

15. 1950 Native Dancer, Social Outcast, Rejected,
Imbros, Dark Star, Straight Face

16. 1966 Majestic Prince, Top Knight, Arts and Letters, Dike,
Al Hattab, Ack Ack

17. 1976 Spectacular Bid, Flying Paster, General Assembly,
Coastal, Golden Act, Czaravich

18. 1986 Sunday Silence, Easy Goer, Black Tie Affair, Twilight
Agenda, Festin, Opening Verse

19. 1989 A.P. Indy, My Memoirs, Pine Bluff,
           Lil E. Tee, Bertrando, Lure

20. 1980 Sunny's Halo, Interco, Play Fellow,
           Desert Wine, Caveat, Slew o' Gold

Top Twenty Female Foal Crops

1. 1970 Desert Vixen, Dahlia, Gay Style

2. 1984 Personal Ensign, Miesque, Bayakoa

3. 1901 Beldame, Hamburg Belle, Dolly Spanker

4. 1903 Brookdale Nymph, Lady Navarre, Running Water

5. 1918 Prudery, Crocus, Bit of White

6. 1966 Gallant Bloom, Ta Wee, Shuvee

7. 1932 Black Helen, Myrtlewood, Good Gamble

8. 1910 Pan Zareta, Flying Fairy, Gowell

9. 1964 Gamely, Princessnesian, Amerigo Lady

10. 1980 Royal Heroine, Estrapade, Princess Rooney

11. 1959 Cicada, Royal Patrice, Old Hat

12. 1944 Conniver, But Why Not, First Flight

13. 1987 Miss Alleged, Go for Wand, Paseana

14. 1947 Next Move, Bed o' Roses, Busanda

15. 1969 Dulcia, Tizna, Susan's Girl

16. 1942 Busher, Gallorette

17. 1972 Ruffian, My Juliet

18. 1902 Artful, Tanya

19. 1952 Misty Morn, Blue Sparkler

20. 1979 All Along, Heatherten

NAMING THE BEST HORSES OF EACH AGE

Some readers might think that all one needs to do is to find out which horses ran the fastest. There are two reasons why this approach is not feasible. In the first place, it doesn't work. You can look at a list of the track record holders at any track, and you will see that the best times were usually posted by horses who were never champions and are in some cases unknown. Times are influenced so much by pace. If the pace happens to be fast, the final time will be fast, even if the field is not particularly strong.

Another reason to abandon time as the ultimate criterion is that it would not be fair to the old-time horses. The entire breed is faster today. There are cheap platers who can run faster than MAN O' WAR did. Does that make them better? You have the same dilemma with human athletes. If Jesse Owens were running and jumping now, he probably could not even qualify for an Olympic team. Does that mean that all of today's Olympic also-rans are greater than Jesse Owens? Clearly, the only fair and reasonable approach is to view each athlete within the context of his own era, and what was possible to achieve at that time.

Let us now consider who the most impressive horses of the century were at each age. We will do the fillies and mares first.

Two-year-old fillies: The all-time most impressive one was TOP FLIGHT. She won all seven of her starts in 1931, all of them stakes. Three times she defeated colts, including future Derby winner BURGOO KING. She even gave away weight to the males. Her season earnings were a record for both sexes – a record that lasted more than twenty years. There have been some freakishly gifted fillies over the years, such as RUFFIAN and LANDALUCE, but they did not have as many starts, nor did they run at all against the boys, nor did they set a money record.

Three-year-old fillies: TWILIGHT TEAR (1944) and BUSHER (1945) were the only two to be voted Horse of the Year at this age during the twentieth century. They both were able to defeat males good enough to be in the Hall of Fame. TWILIGHT TEAR may have an edge because her victim, DEVIL DIVER, was already a champion when she beat him. BUSHER's victim, ARMED, was a new star who possibly had not yet fully blossomed, though this is debatable.

TWILIGHT TEAR's record was 7-1 against fillies and 7-2 against colts. She lost twice at unfair weights, and she lost to older males in February. BUSHER's record was 6-1 against fillies and 4-2 against colts. She did not lose any race in which the weights were fair. BUSHER became the world's leading money-winning female—something TWILIGHT TEAR was unable to achieve even though she had more starts. Which filly was better? You decide. We gave them the same rating.

Four-year-old fillies: If you want perfection, look no farther than PERSONAL ENSIGN. She won all seven of her races in 1988 over a period of six months. BUG BRUSH in 1959 was also outstanding for six months, winning six of her seven starts in California, losing just once by a narrow margin when she got involved in a suicidal pace duel with a lightly weighted male. Her greatest triumph was her victory over the redoubtable HILLSDALE in world-record time. In three races against males, BUG BRUSH made weight concessions quite similar to those made by HILLSDALE, showing that she really was in his league. PERSONAL ENSIGN beat males once, but she did not face a colt as good as HILLSDALE. We are discounting ALL ALONG because her time in the spotlight was so brief.

Five-year-old mares: REGRET, who never raced very often, made four starts in 1917, winning three and losing once by a nose to a lightly weighted male. Ironically, this loss was the greatest performance of her career because so many top colts and geldings finished behind her. WAYA, who was voted champion in 1979, had a spotty record, mostly because of unfair weights. She proved her worth in the Bowling Green Handicap, in which she outran BOWL GAME, the male champion.

Six-year-old mares: The remarkable IMP stands head and shoulders above everyone else. In 1900 she started a mind-boggling 31 times! She won just eight of these races, but one can't really expect such a severely overraced horse to be at her best all the time. Moreover, she often gave away large chunks of weight to decent colts. IMP defeated KINLEY MACK in the Parkway Handicap and ETHELBERT in the Second Special. She also lost to these rivals, but they were two of the best males in the country. The fact that she could run at this level at all, at fair weights, is awe-inspiring. She held eighteen track records.

Two-year-old males: It's a photo finish between COLIN in 1907 and NATIVE DANCER in 1952. Both horses went undefeated, COLIN in twelve races and NATIVE DANCER in nine. COLIN won with 129 pounds; NATIVE DANCER, 126. COLIN set an American record; NATIVE DANCER tied a world mark. NATIVE DANCER set a new earnings record and was voted Horse of the Year in the TRA poll. There were no polls when COLIN ran. Both horses were always considered great ones.

Three-year-old males: MAN O' WAR (1920) has no competition in this division, since he is the only one who excelled in every category by which greatness is measured. SECRETARIAT (1973) was much admired, but he lost too often and did not carry high weight, nor did he set an earning record.

Four-year-old males: There are three contenders here: TOM FOOL (1953), DR FAGER (1968), and SPECTACULAR BID (1980). TOM FOOL and SPECTACULAR BID are the only four-year-olds who completed a full season undefeated. DR. FAGER lost one race in which the weights were unfair.

DR. FAGER won under 139 pounds; TOM FOOL, 136; and SPECTACULAR BID, 132. SPECTACULAR BID had one American record and three track records. DR. FAGER set one world record and two track records. TOM FOOL had two track records. In their best year, DR. FAGER garnered three championships; TOM FOOL, two; and SPECTACULAR BID, one. In addition, all three were Horse of the Year.

Five-year-old males: The protagonists here are SEABISCUIT (1938) and CIGAR (1995). CIGAR is the only horse who went undefeated at this age. SEABISCUIT lost five times, but in every case he was spotting his rivals huge amounts of weight. He won twice under 133 pounds and carried 130 five times. CIGAR never toted more than 126, which seems pretty low for a five-year-old, DISCOVERY having won with 139 when he was only four. SEABISCUIT was called upon to defeat the great WAR ADMIRAL (99.2), while CIGAR's best victims were 95.2 horses like TINNERS WAY and DEVIL HIS DUE. (HOLY BULL does not count because he went lame.) The reader can decide for himself, but we consider SEABISCUIT more impressive.

Six-year-old males: The contenders are WHISK BROOM II (1913) and FOREGO (1976), and your preference is apt to depend on how extensive a campaign you want a horse to have. WHISK BROOM II won all three of his starts, and those three races comprise the Handicap Triple Crown – something FOREGO was never able to win. In the Suburban, WHISK BROOM won in world-record time under 139 pounds. FOREGO's greatest victory, the Marlboro Cup, was won under 137 pounds and just missed the track record on a wet surface. FOREGO put in a full season of eight starts, winning six. In all eight of his starts, he had to concede weight. The average amount he carried was 133 pounds. WHISK BROOM's average was 131.7.

Seven-year-old males: Not many horses are still running at this advanced age, but geldings sometimes do it. The competition is between EXTERMINATOR (1922) and KELSO (1964). EXTERMINATOR won ten of seventeen starts and lugged 138 pounds to victory. KELSO won five of eleven starts, including one triumph under 136. These stats make EXTERMINATOR look better, but KELSO was superior from a time standpoint. KELSO had two American records plus one track record. EXTERMINATOR posted no speed records, even though he had more opportunities to set them.

THE BEST THAT THEY BEAT

In the following listing, horses are ranked according to the quality of the top competitor they beat. We considered "definitive" wins only. For example, we discounted Easy Goer's victory over Sunday Silence because the latter proved in three other races that he was the better horse. We ignored Buckpasser passing Dr. Fager in the Woodward because the latter would never have been ten lengths behind Damascus in a true bill. Here's how forty great horses finished:

1.	Seattle Slew	14.	Devil Diver	27.	Forego
2.	Affirmed	15.	Armed	28.	Round Table
3.	Dr. Fager	16.	Shut Out	29.	Gallant Fox
4.	Damascus	17.	Whirlaway	30.	Spectacular Bid
5.	Swaps	18.	Discovery	31.	Sysonby
6.	Nashua	19.	Man o' War	32.	Assault
7.	Seabiscuit	20.	Equipoise	33.	Cigar
8.	Bold Ruler	21.	Kelso	34.	War Admiral
9.	Gallant Man	22.	Secretariat	35.	Alydar
10.	Sunday Silence	23.	Colin	36.	Easy Goer
11.	Cavalcade	24.	Old Rosebud	37.	Count Fleet
12.	Twilight Tear (F.)	25.	Cudgel	38.	Tom Fool
13.	Busher (F.)	26.	Citation	39.	Buckpasser
				40.	Native Dancer

CITATION, CALUMET FARM, AND SWAPS

Some historians have claimed that CITATION was "never the same horse," following his injury of 1949. We do not share this view at all. CITATION actually ran faster when he was "not himself" than he ever had run when he <u>was</u> himself! Just imagine what CITATION'S 1950 season would have been like, if his nemesis NOOR had stayed in England:

1. The various speed records attributed to NOOR would have been CITATION'S records, added to the one world record that he actually did set.
2. Instead of a dismal 2-7 season, his record would have been 6-3, quite respectable in the handicap division.
3. He would have won the Santa Anita Handicap under 132 pounds, which has never been done.
4. He would have become racing's first millionaire in 1950 instead of 1951.

With credentials like these, CITATION would have been voted Horse of the Year all over again. He would have been hailed as the same great champion that he always was. It's a shame that NOOR spoiled things for him at unfair weights.

It's only our opinion, but we believe that CITATION'S early losses in 1951 were a deliberate strategy to keep his weight down for the lucrative Hollywood Gold Cup. The plan worked, and he went to the post under the ridiculous weight of 120 pounds. Naturally, he won easily. We also believe that Calumet Farm had a policy of not allowing their horses to win under more than 130 pounds. Call us cynical if you like, but we think it is just too much of a coincidence that neither WHIRLAWAY nor ARMED nor COALTOWN ever won with more than 130. Every time they were assigned 132 pounds, they lost. Had they won under that impost, they would have had to continue to carry that much, if not more. By losing, they would get dropped back down to 130. The lone exception to this would be the 1950 Santa Anita Handicap. Since CITATION was seeking a money record, Calumet presumably did want to win that race.

Rex Ellsworth, the owner of SWAPS, refused to run his steed under more than 130 pounds. Since SWAPS was a huge box office attraction at Hollywood Park, management naturally wanted the great horse to perform. Since they couldn't raise the weight on SWAPS, they kept lowering the weights on his rivals. The situation became so absurd that, in the Sunset Handicap, all of SWAPS' opponents went to the post overweight because their riders could not make the low weights that were assigned. SWAPS won the race laughing, as usual. We believe Ellsworth's attitude was understandable. SWAPS suffered a life-threatening injury in 1956. Probably realizing all along that his superstar was fragile, he must have worried that excessive weight might cause his horse to break down. SWAPS did recover from his injury and went on to become a successful sire.

Top Jockeys and Their Best Mounts

EDDIE ARCARO

Whirlaway
Citstion
Nashua
Bold Ruler
Kelso

STEVE CAUTHEN

Affirmed

ANGEL CORDERO, JR.

Bold Forbes
Seattle Slew
Waya
Relaxing
Slew o' Gold
Spend a Buck

JEAN CRUGUET

Hoist the Flag
Seattle Slew
Mac Diarmida

PAT DAY

Vanlandingham
Easy Goer
Paradise Creek
Favorite Trick

EDDIE DELAHOUSSAYE

Risen Star
A.P. Indy
Hollywood Wildcat

KENT DESORMEAUX

Kotashaan
Real Quiet

ERIC GUERIN

Next Move
Native Dancer
Berlo

BILL HARTACK

Fabius
Iron Liege
Tim Tam
Royal Native
Northern Dancer
Majestic Prince

JOHNNY LONGDEN

Count Fleet
Busher
Noor

EDDIE MAPLE

Temperence Hill
Conquistador Cielo
Swale

CHRIS McCARRON

John Henry
Precisionist
Alysheba
Miss Alleged
Flawlessly

LAFFIT PINCAY, JR.

Affirmed
Althea
Swale
Bayakoa

RED POLLARD

Seabiscuit

RANDY ROMERO

Personal Ensign
Go for Wand

EARL SANDE

Grey Lag
Zev
Sarazen
Crusader
Gallant Fox

BILL SHOEMAKER

Swaps
Gallant Man
Round Table
Sword Dancer
Jaipur
Cicada
Candy Spots
Lucky Debonair
Damascus
Ack Ack
Cougar II
Forego
Exceller
Spectacular Bid
John Henry
Ferdinand

MIKE SMITH

Lure
Sky Beauty
Holy Bull
Inside Information

ALEX SOLIS

Snow Chief
Bertrando

GARY STEVENS

Winning Colors
Serena's Song
Silver Charm

RON TURCOTTE

Riva Ridge
Secretariat

ISMAEL VALENZUELA

Tim Tam
Kelso

PAT VALENZUELA

Sunday Silence

JACINTO VASQUEZ

Foolish Pleasure
Ruffian
Genuine Risk

JORGE VELASQUEZ

Fort Marcy
Desert Vixen
Chris Evert
Alydar
Davona Dale
Pleasant Colony

GEORGE WOOLF

Seabiscuit
Challedon
Whirlaway

Drew Slater

MANUEL YCAZA

Bald Eagle
Never Bend
Quadrangle
Ack Ack

TOP TRAINERS AND
THEIR BEST PUPILS

BOB BAFFERT

Silver Charm
Real Quiet

LAZ BARRERA

Bold Forbes
Affirmed

ELLIOT BURCH

Sword Dancer
Arts and Letters
Fort Marcy
Key to the Mint

E. A. CHRISTMAS

Challedon
Gallorette
Berlo

JAMES FITZSIMMONS

Gallant Fox

Omaha
Granville
Johnstown
Nashua
Bold Ruler

JOHN GAVER

Shut Out
Devil Diver
Capot
Tom Fool
The Axe II
Stage Door Johnny

T. J. HEALY

Top Flight
Equipoise

WARREN CROLL, JR.

Housebuster
Holy Bull

NEIL DRYSDALE

Princess Rooney
A. P. Indy
Hollywood Wildcat

L. FENSTERMAKER

Susan's Girl
Precisionist

LEROY JOLLEY

Foolish Pleasure
Honest Pleasure
Genuine Risk
Manila

BEN A. JONES

Whirlaway
Twilight Tear

SAM HILDRETH

Fitz Herbert
Friar Rock
Hourless
Mad Hatter
Grey Lag
Zev

MAX HIRSCH

Sarazen
Bold Venture
Assault
High Gun

HIRSCH JACOBS

Stymie
Affectionately

RON McANALLY

John Henry
Bayakoa

BEN A. JONES

Armed
Real Delight

H. A. "JIMMY" JONES

Bewitch
Citation
Coaltown
Two Lea
Gen. Duke
Iron Liege
Tim Tam

LUCIEN LAURIN

Riva Ridge
Secretariat

D. WAYNE LUKAS

Althea
Lady's Secret
Winning Colors
Criminal Type
Serena's Song

SHUG McGAUGHEY

Vanlandingham
Personal Ensign
Easy Goer
Lure
Heavenly Prize
Inside Information

BILL MOTT

Paradise Creek
Cigar
Favorite Trick

W. F. MULHOLLAND

Battlefield
Jaipur

EDDIE NELOY

Gun Bow
Buckpasser

D. WAYNE LUKAS

Charismatic

JAMES ROWE, SR.

Commando
Sysonby
Colin
Maskette
Whisk Broom II
Regret

FLINT SCHULHOFER

Ta Wee
Mac Diarmida

WOODY STEPHENS

Bald Eagle

Never Bend
Conquistador Cielo
Swale
Forty Niner

JOHN NERUD

Gallant Man
Intentionally
Dr. Fager

SYLVESTER VEITCH

First Flight
Counterpoint

P. D. WEIR

Roseben
Old Rosebud

R. L. WHEELER

Bug Brush
Silver Spoon

FRANK WHITELEY, JR.

Damascus
Ruffian
Forego

M. A. TENNEY

Swaps
Prove It
Candy Spots

JACK VAN BERG

Gate Dancer
Alysheba

JOHN VEITCH

Alydar
Davona Dale

CHARLIE WHITTINGHAM

Cougar II
Ack Ack
Dahlia
Exceller
Ferdinand
Sunday Silence
Flawlessly

W. C. WINFREY

Next Move
Native Dancer
Social Outcast

LEADING OWNERS

BELAIR STUD

Gallant Fox
Omaha
Granville
Johnstown
Nashua
Exceller

AUGUST BELMONT II

Beldame
Fair Play
Friar Rock
Hourless

E. R. BRADLEY

Blue Larkspur
Black Helen
Bimelech

CALUMET FARM

Bull Lea
Whirlaway
Pensive

Twilight Tear
Armed
Fervent
Bewitch
Citation
Coaltown
Ponder
Two Lea
Real Delight
Mark-Ye-Well
Fabius
Gen. Duke
Iron Liege
Bardstown
Tim Tam
Alydar
Davona Dale
Criminal Type

W. L. BRANN

Challedon
Gallorette

BROOKMEADE STABLE

Cavalcade
Sword Dancer

CAIN HOY STABLE

Dark Star
Bald Eagle
Never Bend
Ack Ack

REX C. ELLSWORTH

Swaps
Prove It
Candy Spots

MR. & MRS. FIRESTONE

Honest Pleasure
Genuine Risk

CLAIBORNE FARM

Swale
Forty Niner
Lure

A. J. CREVOLIS CO.

Imbros
Determine

DARBY DAN FARM

Chateaugay
Little Current

MRS. JOHN D. HERTZ

Reigh Count
Count Fleet

SAM HILDRETH

King James
Fitz Herbert

FOXCATCHER FARM

Rosemont
Berlo

GREENTREE STABLE

Twenty Grand
Shut Out
Devil Diver
Capot
Tom Fool
The Axe II
Stage Door Johnny

HARBOR VIEW FARM

Roman Brother
Affirmed
Flawlessly

W. G. HELIS, JR.

Spartan Valor
Helioscope

FRED W. HOOPER

Olympia
Susan's Girl
Precisionist

CHARLES S. HOWARD

Seabiscuit
Mioland
Noor

NELSON B. HUNT

Dahlia
Exceller

ETHEL D. JACOBS

Marriage
Stymie
Affectionately

JAMES R. KEENE

Commando
Sysonby
Colin
Maskette
Iron Mask

W. S. KILMER

Exterminator
Sun Beau

KING RANCH

Assault
But Why Not
Rejected
High Gun
Gallant Bloom
Canonero II

EUGENE KLEIN

Lady's Secret
Winning Colors

MR. & MRS. JEFFORDS

Pavot
One Count

LOUIS B. MAYER

Busher
Honeymoon

MEADOW STABLE

Hill Prince
Sir Gaylord
Cicada
Riva Ridge
Secretariat

W. H. PERRY

Gamely
Tiller

BOB & BEVERLY LEWIS

Serena's Song
Silver Charm
Charismatic

LOBLOLLY STABLE

Temperence Hill
Vanlandingham

SAMUEL D. RIDDLE

Man o' War

Crusader
War Admiral

ROKEBY TABLE

Quadrangle
Arts and Letters
Fort Marcy
Key to the Mint

OGDEN PHIPPS

Buckpasser
Relaxing
Personal Ensign
Easy Goer
Heavenly Prize

RANCOCAS STABLE

Mad Hatter
Grey Lag
Zev

B. J. RIDDER

Cascapedia
Flying Paster

C. V. WHITNEY

Top Flight
Equipoise
First Flight
Counterpoint
Bug Brush
Silver Spoon

Quicken Tree

J. K. L. ROSS

Cudgel
Sir Barton

S. SOMMER

Autobiography
Sham

TARTAN STABLE

Dr. Fager
Ta Wee

ALFRED G. VANDERBILT

Discovery
Next Move
Native Dancer
Social Outcast

H. P. WHITNEY

Artful
Tanya
Whisk Broom II
Regret
Johren
John P. Grier
Prudery
Equipoise

GEORGE D. WIDENER

Jack High
Jamestown
Eight Thirty
Lucky Draw
Battlefield
Jaipur

THE 100 GREATEST RACES OF THE CENTURY AND WHO WON

For this list we have chosen the horses either for the quality of their performance or the quality of the competition they faced. Rare occurrences and close finishes are often included.

1901   Carlton Stakes: COMMANDO. He concedes fifteen lbs. to a quality opponent, Blues.

1904   White Plains H: ARTFUL. She sets world record at two under 130 pounds.

1905   Belmont S: TANYA. Century's only female Belmont winner.

1908   Tidal S: COLIN. Wins his final race and retires undefeated.

1913   Suburban H: WHISK BROOM II. World record under 139 lbs. Sweeps Handicap Triple Crown.

1914   sprint at Juarez: IRON MASK. New world record under 150 lbs.

1915   Kentucky Derby: REGRET. First ever filly Derby winner.

1917   Delaware H: OLD ROSEBUD. Totes 133 lbs, defeats Roamer (127).

1917   Match Race at Laurel: HOURLESS. Beats Omar Khayyam. New track record.

1918   Brooklyn H: CUDGEL. Roamer finishes second, George Smith third.

1918   Travers S: SUN BRIAR. Beats Johren, War Cloud and Exterminator.

1918   Bowie H: GEORGE SMITH. Omar Khayyam second, Exterminator third. New track record under 130 lbs.

1919   Havre de Grace H: CUDGEL. Exterminator runs second, Sir Barton third.

1920   Dwyer S: MAN O' WAR. New American record. Spots John P. Grier eighteen lbs. in match race.

1920   Saratoga H: SIR BARTON. Defeats Exterminator. New track record.

1920   Merchants & Citizens H: SIR BARTON. New world record under 133 lbs.

1920   Lawrence Realization: MAN O' WAR. 100-length massacre. New world record.

1920   Potomac H: MAN O' WAR. Wins at three under 138 lbs. New track record.

1921   Devonshire International: GREY LAG. New Canadian record. Noses out Black Servant.

1922   Brooklyn H: EXTERMINATOR. 135 lbs., conceding nine to Grey Lag. Wins by a head.

1924   International Special #3: SARAZEN. Beats all-star field in blazing time.

1930   Kentucky Jockey Club S: TWENTY GRAND. Defeats Equipoise by a nose in record time.

1932   handicap at Arlington Park: EQUIPOISE. World-record win, conceding ten lbs. to Jamestown.

1934   Preakness: HIGH QUEST. Cavalcade finishes second and Discovery third. Wins by a nose

1934   American Derby: CAVALCADE. Concedes eight lbs. to Discovery.

1935   Brooklyn H: DISCOVERY. Defeats Omaha by twelve lengths in record time.

1935   Detroit Challenge Cup: DISCOVERY. Wins by thirty lengths. Equals track record.

1935   Merchants & Citizens H: DISCOVERY. Wins at age four under 139 lbs.

1936   Preakness: BOLD VENTURE. A nose victory over rival Granville.

1937 Belmont S: WAR ADMIRAL. Hurts himself, wins anyway. Equals American record. Sweeps Triple Crown.

1938 Santa Anita H: STAGEHAND. Noses out Seabiscuit. Pompoon third. New track record.

1938 Pimlico Special: SEABISCUIT. Four-length Match Race win vs. War Admiral. New track record.

1940 Santa Anita H: SEABISCUIT. He finally wins big race, sets new earnings record.

1941 Jockey Club Gold Cup: MARKET WISE. Noses out Whirlaway in American-record time.

1942 Phoenix H: DEVIL DIVER. Defeats Whirlaway by a diminishing head.

1942 Match Race at Narragansett: ALSAB. Prevails by a nose over closing Whirlaway.

1942 Champagne S: COUNT FLEET. Fastest mile ever by a two-year-old.

1943 Belmont S: COUNT FLEET. Victorious by twenty-five lengths. Sweeps Triple Crown.

1944 Pimlico Special: TWILIGHT TEAR. She beats older male champ Devil Diver.

1945 Suburban H: DEVIL DIVER. Vanquishes Stymie, spotting him thirteen pounds. Carries 132 lbs.

1945   Washington Park H: BUSHER. She defeats older male star
        Armed. New track record.

1947   Butler H: ASSAULT. Wins by a head under 135 lbs. Stymie
        (126) is second, Gallorette (117) third.

1949   Whirlaway S: COALTOWN. Posts new world record.
        Ponder second.

1949   Sysonby Mile: CAPOT. Whips Coaltown in major slugfest.

1950   allowance at Santa Anita: CITATION. A record sixteenth
        consecutive victory.

1950   San Juan Capistrano: NOOR. Noses out Citation in
        thrilling duel. New world record.

1951   Hollywood Gold Cup: CITATION. Becomes the first
        millionaire in racing history.

1952   Jockey Club Gold Cup: ONE COUNT. Mark-Ye-Well
        second, Crafty Admiral third in major showdown.

1953   Brooklyn H: TOM FOOL. Completes Handicap Triple
        Crown sweep. Shoulders 136 lbs.

1954   Metropolitan H: NATIVE DANCER. Scores by a neck
        after brilliant stretch run.

1954   Arlington Classic: ERRARD KING. Helioscope finishes
        second, High Gun third.

1955 Kentucky Derby: SWAPS. California star defeats the king of the east, Nashua.

1955 Match Race at Washinton Park: NASHUA. He whips Swaps. They never met again.

1956 Suburban H: NASHUA. Concedes seventeen lbs. to talented Dedicate.

1956 American H: SWAPS. Fifth of his six world records. Concedes 19 lbs. to Mister Gus.

1956 Jockey Club Gold Cup: NASHUA. New American record. Wins stake for second time.

1957 Florida Derby: GEN. DUKE. Equals world record in victory over Bold Ruler. Iron Liege third.

1957 Belmont S: GALLANT MAN. New American record. Tallies by eight lengths. Bold Ruler third.

1957 Ben Franklin H: BOLD RULER. Scores by twelve lengths. Totes 136 lbs. at three.

1957 Trenton H: BOLD RULER. Gallant Man second, Round Table third in showdown race.

1958 Suburban H: BOLD RULER. Nose victory under 134 lbs. Concedes 25 lbs. to Clem.

1959 San Antonio H: BUG BRUSH. She defeats Hillsdale, posts new world record.

1959   Arlington H: ROUND TABLE. A new American record under 132 lbs.

1959   Woodward S: SWORD DANCER. Beats Hillsdale by a head. Round Table third in climactic face-off.

1961   Brooklyn H: KELSO. Completes Handicap Triple Crown sweep under 136 lbs.

1962   Travers S: JAIPUR. Nips archrival Ridan by a nose. Equals track record.

1964   Monmouth H: MONGO. Defeats Kelso by a neck. Gun Bow finishes third in major confrontation.

1964   Woodward S: GUN BOW. Upsets the mighty Kelso by a nose.

1964   Jockey Club Gold Cup: KELSO. Fifth straight win in this stake. Breaks his own American record.

1966   Santa Anita H: LUCKY DEBONAIR. First Derby winner to capture race. Beats Native Diver, Hill Rise.

1966   Arlington Classic: BUCKPASSER. New world record because of lightning - fast pace plus his great talent.

1967   Travers S: DAMASCUS. Romps home by twenty-two lengths. Equals track record.

1967   Woodward S: DAMASCUS. Trounces Buckpasser by ten lengths. Dr. Fager third in "Race of the Decade."

1968   Suburban H: DR. FAGER. Whips Damascus by five lengths. Equals track record.

1968   Washington Park H. DR. FAGER. World record under 134 lbs. Scores by ten lengths.

1968   United Nations H: DR. FAGER. Shoulders 134 lbs. Concedes sixteen lbs. to grass champion Fort Marcy.

1969   Kentucky Derby: MAJESTIC PRINCE. Beats Arts and Letters a neck. Dike third.

1973   Belmont S: SECRETARIAT. 31-length victory in world-record time. Sweeps Triple Crown.

1973   Brooklyn H: RIVA RIDGE. Originally a world record. Became American standard for decades.

1973   Beldame S: DESERT VIXEN. Equals American record. Beats Susan's Girl by almost twelve lengths.

1973   Marlboro Cup: SECRETARIAT. World-record victory over Riva Ridge. Cougar II third.

1973   Jockey Club Gold Cup: PROVE OUT. Outsprints Riva Ridge, outstays the rest.

1976   Marlboro Cup: FOREGO. Lugs 137 lbs., beats Honest Pleasure (119) by a head.

1977   Belmont S: SEATTLE SLEW. The first to sweep Triple Crown while still unbeaten.

1978   Belmont S: AFFIRMED. Wins Triple Crown by a head over archrival Alydar.

1978   Marlboro Cup: SEATTLE SLEW. Beats Affirmed by three lengths. First-ever clash of Triple Crown winners.

1978   Jockey Club Gold Cup: EXCELLER. Edges Seattle Slew by a nose. Makes up twenty-two lengths.

1979   Jockey Club Gold Cup: AFFIRMED. Vanquishes Spectacular Bid by ¾ of a length in clash of titans.

1980   Strub S: SPECTACULAR BID. New American record on dirt. Flying Paster second.

1980   San Luis Rey S: JOHN HENRY. Gallant gelding equals the world record.

1980   Kentucky Derby: GENUINE RISK. First filly in sixty-five years to capture the Derby.

1983   Super Derby: SUNNY'S HALO. Scores ten-length victory over Play Fellow.

1987   Strub S: SNOW CHIEF. Defeats Ferdinand by a nose in thrilling finish. Broad Brush third.

1988   Kentucky Derby: WINNING COLORS. Third and last filly to score in the Derby.

1988   Breeders' Cup Distaff: PERSONAL ENSIGN. Nails Winning Colors by a nose. Retires undefeated.

1989   Gotham S: EASY GOER. Thirteen-length win is fastest mile ever by a three-year-old.

1989   Breeders' Cup Classic: SUNDAY SILENCE. Defeats Easy Goer by a neck in climactic showdown.

1996   Citation Challenge Cup: CIGAR. Ties record of sixteen consecutive victories.

1997   Preakness: SILVER CHARM. Beats Free House and Captain Bodgit in blanket finish.

1998   Breeders' Cup Classic: AWESOME AGAIN. Whips Silver Charm and an all-star field.

LOCATION OF RACES

49	New York
11	California
10	Illinois
10	Kentucky
9	Maryland
4	New Jersey
2	Florida
1	Rhode Island
1	Michigan
1	Louisiana
1	Mexico
1	Canada
–––	
100	

Frequency In Top 100

7	Jockey Club Gold Cup
7	Belmont S.
6	Brooklyn H.
5	Suburban H.
5	Kentucky Derby
3	Marlboro Cup
3	Woodward S.
3	Santa Anita H.
3	Preakness S.
3	Travers S.
2	Breeders' Cup Classic
2	Pimlico Special
2	Strub S.
2	Merchants & Citizens H.
2	Washington Park H.
2	Arlington Classic

THE MOST REMARKABLE RACES:

New York:

1. 1920 Lawrence Realization
2. 1973 Belmont S.
3. 1913 Suburban H.
4. 1908 Tidal S.
5. 1943 Belmont S.
6. 1978 Belmont S.
7. 1937 Belmont S.
8. 1978 Marlboro Cup
9. 1935 Merchants & Citizens
10. 1967 Woodward S.
11. 1979 Jockey Club Gold Cup
12. 1904 White Plains H.
13. 1967 Travers S.
14. 1961 Brooklyn H.
15. 1953 Brooklyn H.
16. 1977 Belmont S.
17. 1920 Merchants & Citizens
18. 1958 Suburban H.
19. 1976 Marlboro Cup
20. 1922 Brooklyn H.
21. 1956 Suburban H.
22. 1935 Brooklyn H.
23. 1905 Belmont S.
24. 1968 Suburban H.
25. 1945 Suburban H.

26. 1947 Butler H.
27. 1973 Marlboro Cup
28. 1973 Brooklyn H.
29. 1920 Dwyer S.
30. 1941 Jockey Club Gold Cup

CALIFORNIA:

1. 1950 allowance, Jan. 11
2. 1956 American H.
3. 1951 Hollywood Gold Cup
4. 1959 San Antonio H.
5. 1950 San Juan Capistrano
6. 1980 San Luis Rey S.
7. 1980 Strub S.
8. 1940 Santa Anita H.
9. 1938 Santa Anita H.
10. 1987 Strub S.

ILLINOIS:

1. 1968 Washington Park H.
2. 1996 Citation Challenge Cup
3. 1955 Match Race
4. 1959 Arlington H.
5. 1932 handicap, June 30
6. 1949 Whirlaway S.
7. 1966 Arlington Classic
8. 1945 Washington Park H.
9. 1954 Arlington Classic
10. 1934 American Derby

KENTUCKY:

1. 1988 Breeders' Cup Distaff
2. 1924 International Special #3
3. 1930 Kentucky Jockey Club S.

4. 1915 Kentucky Derby
5. 1988 Kentucky Derby
6. 1980 Kentucky Derby
7. 1955 Kentucky Derby
8. 1998 Breeders' Cup Classic
9. 1969 Kentucky Derby
10. 1942 Phoenix H.

MARYLAND:

1. 1920 Potomac H.
2. 1938 Pimlico Special
3. 1944 Pimlico Special
4. 1934 Preakness
5. 1919 Havre de Grace H.
6. 1918 Bowie H.
7. 1917 Match Race
8. 1936 Preakness
9. 1997 Preakness
10. 1978 Preakness

OTHER STATES:

1. 1914 sprint, March 8, (Mexico)
2. 1957 Ben Franklin H. (New Jersey)
3. 1935 Detroit Challenge Cup (Michigan)
4. 1968 United Nations H. (New Jersey)
5. 1957 Trenton H. (New Jersey)
6. 1989 Breeders' Cup Classic (Florida)
7. 1964 Monmouth H. (New Jersey)
8. 1957 Florida Derby (Florida)
9. 1942 Match Race (Rhode Island)
10. 1921 Devonshire International (Canada)

FREQUENCY IN TOP 100

Aughts	4
Teens	9
Twenties	8
Thirties	11
Forties	12
Fifties	20
Sixties	13
Seventies	11
Eighties	9
Nineties	3
100 races	

TEN WAYS TO IMPROVE HORSE RACING IN AMERICA

1. Horses need to run more often. It's hard to have a thriving sport when its top stars hardly ever perform. Decades ago, there were major confrontations every few weeks. Today's trainers are ruining the sport by keeping their best runners in the barn. There should be a rule that horses (except for juveniles) are not eligible for Eclipse Awards unless they have had at least eight starts that year.

2. Horses should go back to carrying more weight, the way they used to. Today's "handicaps" are a complete farce. The top horse may hoist as little as seven or eight pounds more than the bottom horse. This is not enough of a weight spread to bring these two horses to the finish line together, which is the goal. Moreover, the Scale of Weights should be printed in every program.

3. Purses for filly and mare races should be reduced. The public enjoys seeing the best females take on the males, but it seldom happens anymore because there are so many lucrative opportunities exclusively for fillies and mares. In olden days, top females ran against males nearly all the time because they could make more money doing that.

4. Slash the number of Breeders' Cup races back down to seven events. Right now, there are so many cup races that there is no longer any focus or clarity. Some of the races do not even attract Grade I fields. The entire presentation has become far too unwieldy and diluted.

5. Some tracks ought to close. Obviously this idea would sink like a lead balloon within the industry, but it would be a good thing for fans. Nowadays there are so many tracks open at the same time that it is quite easy for the best horses to duck one another. In the first four months of 2014, for example, there was only one race—the Santa Anita Handicap – that attracted the best horses in the country. No wonder the general public has lost interest in racing.

6. <u>Daily Racing Form</u> should stop spoon-feeding so much information to the public. Handicapping was a lot more fun in the olden days when you were largely on your own in figuring out how good each horse was. All you got in those days were the basic past performances and the selections of five experts. Whatever else you wanted, such as speed figures, you had to make yourself. Those were the days!

7. Eliminate synthetic surfaces. Some tracks are already doing this. Research has shown that, although some kinds of injuries were reduced, other kinds became more frequent than ever. Synthetic tracks favor grass horses over dirt horses, and closers over front runners. They don't provide outcomes that are true or fair for all the participants.

8. Medication rules should be just as strict in America as they are in Europe. Any kind of steroid or performance-enhancing drug should be universally banned. Many people don't follow racing because they don't consider it honest. We believe that colts are often given some kind of steroid or drug that fillies don't receive. That would explain why modern females are just as good as they ever were, but males have deteriorated noticeably since 1980.

9. Experiment with the dates of the Triple Crown jewels. Many younger people don't know that the spacing of the races was not always the same as it is today. Modern trainers, who are loath to race their horses, always say they would like more time between the events. However, we believe just the opposite would result in more Triple Crown winners, because a hot horse would be more likely to hold his top form over a shorter number of weeks, before he starts to tail off.

10. For televised races, hire proven experts to analyze each event. They should be professional horse players–not merely sports reporters. Racing fans would welcome the opportunity to learn from true authorities, but these experts would need to be forthcoming about the reasons why they like or dislike certain horses. With all due respect to Jerry Bailey and Gary Stevens, jockeys are seldom great handicappers. We would be better off hearing from their agents! In recent years, NBC has improved in this regard.

Concerning Weight

Many of today's professional handicappers will tell you that weight is not important. Perhaps it's a little less important than it used to be, since today's horses carry such ridiculously low weights in most major races. Handicaps have become a complete joke. The top-weighted older horse often carries only 118 or 119 pounds—much less than he toted when he was only three—and slightly less than he probably carried when he was only two! The top impost should be at least 128 pounds. As for the lowest impost, it can't be much lower than 112 pounds because jockeys, who are already starving themselves, cannot make weights lower than that. Back in the olden days, the bottom horse could be assigned 97 pounds, and there were riders who could make that weight! Those days are gone.

Despite what you may have heard, weight is still very important. Horses like FOREGO and KELSO, who could spot their opponents huge poundage, are extremely rare. Most animals cannot even concede five pounds, and some cannot concede even four pounds! If it surprises you that so little weight can matter, remember the old adage: four pounds equal one length in a sprint, and two pounds equal one length over a route distance. Whenever you try to interpret a race result, always consider weight. Our rule of thumb is as follows: If the impost of the winner is less than that of the runner-up by five pounds or more, the better horse is the one with the higher weight. If the difference is three pounds or less, the better horse is the one that won. A difference of four pounds is difficult to read. It is best to consider the two horses equal for the time being. Eventually, later race results will tell you which horse must have been better. Once in a while, the racing secretary makes a mistake, and the weight assignments are simply wrong. Again, later race results will enable you to figure this out.

CONCERNING SPEED AND TIME

Today's professional handicappers—and their many followers—are obsessed with speed figures. They seem to think that horses are cars, and all you have to do is figure out the velocity of each car. But horses are not cars. They are flesh and blood, and they have different personalities and temperaments that affect the way they run. Some horses are highly energetic. They love to run. They push themselves hard all the way around the track, setting or forcing the pace. This is apt to result in a fast time.

Some other horses are highly lethargic. They will do what they have to do in order to win—but no more. They dawdle behind a pace set by others. If it's not a particularly fast pace, a lot of time may elapse before a lethargic horse even begins to run hard, which he may need to do for only a few furlongs, then coasting the rest of the way home. This is apt to result in a slower time.

Speed handicappers tend to believe that energetic horses, because they run in faster times, are better than lethargic horses—but often this is not really true. Back in the forties, energetic horses were called "hot," and lethargic horses were called "cold." COALTOWN was considered a hot horse, and CITATION was considered a cold horse. Yet we all know that CITATION was a better horse than COALTOWN. If you are totally addicted to comparing times, it would be wiser to compare only horses who have the same running style. We did this, and we discovered that RUFFIAN did not run as fast as BOLD FORBES.

One of the oddities of racing—one which surely must cause speed handicappers to tear their hair out—is that good horses often lose in faster time than they win! For example, when MAN O' WAR lost at six furlongs to UPSET, the time was faster than MAN O' WAR ever won at that distance—and he won five times at six furlongs. Even when he won on a <u>straight</u> course, his time was still slower than UPSET's! When WHIRLAWAY lost at 1 1/2 miles to BOLINGBROKE, the time was more than three seconds faster than WHIRLAWAY's win at that distance. Yet it is universally known that WHIRLAWAY was a much better horse than BOLINGBROKE—just as MAN O' WAR was a much better horse than UPSET.

When a good horse is losing, he puts up a tremendous fight all the way to the wire, thereby pushing his conqueror to a very fast time. When the good horse wins, he can zoom to the front quickly and then slow down and just coast to victory. Some horses are versatile enough to change their running style. When CANONERO II won the Kentucky Derby, he came from behind and scored in slow time. Then, in the Preakness, he ran on the pace all the way, and his winning time was a new track record. Same horse, different scenario. The suitability of the distance also affects the time. BOLD FORBES ran the first ten furlongs of the Belmont in almost the same fast time that he had won the Derby. However, the final time of the Belmont was rather slow because he was not really a distance horse and was tiring at the end.

CONCERNING MARGINS

Many racing fans are impressed by a wide margin of victory, but they really shouldn't be. Margins can be very deceptive. ALYDAR upset AFFIRMED by 3 ½ lengths and by 1 1/4 lengths, whereas AFFIRMED beat ALYDAR five times by half a length or less. Only twice did he whip ALYDAR by wider margins than that. NATIVE DANCER defeated JAMIE K. by only a neck in both the Preakness and the Belmont. However, in the Metropolitan Mile, he outran JAMIE K. by more than six lengths. This happened because he was facing a better horse–STRAIGHT FACE–whom he beat by a neck. Another great horse, BUCKPASSER, won fifteen times by less than one length. He got the job done, and there was no reason for him to win by a wide margin.

A small margin of victory is more apt to be a true indicator of which is the best horse in a race. It shows that the race was competitive, that each contender had a good chance to win if he was good enough. When the margin is wide, it may mean that the runner-up was not "running his race." Perhaps he didn't sleep well, or perhaps he just didn't feel like exerting himself that day. A situation like this developed in 1964. In the Whitney Handicap, GUN BOW trounced MONGO by ten lengths. Many people interpreted this to mean that GUN BOW was a much better horse. Yet the two animals met on three other occasions that year, and every time MONGO defeated his rival. MONGO also was better than GUN BOW at upsetting KELSO.

One of the best scenarios that indicates a true, authentic race result occurs when the victory margin is small, but there is a big gap between the second horse and the third horse. This happened four times to AFFIRMED and ALYDAR, with AFFIRMED winning every time.

A race like this shows that the first two horses were giving it everything they had, pulling away from the third horse. However, it doesn't always mean that the first two horses are close together in ability, nor does it prove that the third horse is substantially inferior. He may have simply given up the chase.

CONCERNING CLASS

What is the best way to measure class? It's not time, it's not earnings, and it's not consistency, although these factors can provide clues. The best method is to look at what happened when horses actually ran against each other. Such head-to-head clashes are the basis of the numerical ratings provided in this book. That is why we have been careful to mention, throughout this book, which horses beat which other horses.

Always remember, when interpreting a race result, to note the weights carried. All racing fans should have a copy of the Scale of Weights, but hardly any do. This scale shows what weight a three-year-old is expected to be able to carry against his elders at different distances in different months. Suppose the difference between the youngster and his elders is considered to be eight pounds. Just add eight to the weight he was assigned for the race, and that tells you what he was <u>really</u> carrying in relation to his elders.

Do a similar thing with fillies and mares. A female is entitled to carry five pounds less than the boys until September 1. After that, she gets three pounds off. Therefore, add the five (or the three) to the weight she was assigned, and that tells you what she truly toted. Anyone who did this for the 1990 Santa Anita Handicap figured out that BAYAKOA had no chance. Yet she went postward the favorite anyway because most bettors never factor in weight. She finished last.

Horse-versus-horse comparisons are only useful for stakes races. You can't apply the method to claiming events. In the first place, there are so many cheap horses that it would be impossible to keep track of them all. Secondly, such animals are so inconsistent that it would be difficult to discern many patterns. But you shouldn't be betting on such races anyway. In today's OTB world, you have an ample supply of stakes events every weekend. For each division that you choose to follow, you will have only about seventy horses to keep track of, and they only run once a month at most.

Concerning Wagering

A great many racing fans put a lot of time and effort into their handicapping, but they never give any thought to their betting. The latter deserves just as much attention. We recommend that you do all of your handicapping the night before you go to the track. Then, when you get there, you have nothing left to do but to watch the tote board and contemplate how you think you ought to bet the race.

The worst mistake so many racing fans make is that they bet far too many races. Suppose there are ten races and you have fifty dollars to spend. If you wager five dollars to win on every race, you will not make much money even if some of your horses come in. Instead, bet the whole fifty on one horse, or perhaps $25 each on two horses. You'll make a lot more money if you're right, and your chances of winning will be better because you'll only be betting on your best opportunities.

It is mathematically certain that you can't come out ahead at the races in the long run unless you wager on overlays. An overlay is a horse whose true chances are better than his odds suggest. Come to the track with your own estimates of what you believe the odds ought to be. If you're confident about a certain horse, but you don't think his odds are fair, skip the race. If you like two different overlays in the same race, bet them both.

Exotic wagers are risky. You need to be very confident if you're going to bet that way. In a mythical ten-horse field in which every horse has a decent chance, you have one chance in ten of picking the winner. Yet you have only one chance in ninety of hitting the exacta, and only one chance in 720 of hitting the trifecta! Of course, a smart bettor would never play a race in which every horse had an equal chance.

Finally, let us remind racing fans that your handicapping can affect your betting outcomes. If you are a speed handicapper like so many others, you will pick the same horses as everyone else—and that will spoil the odds on your winners. If you base your system on something else—such as class—you will get better odds, more overlays and greater profits. Good luck!

Printed in the United States
By Bookmasters